Airline TOEIC Intro

Airline TOEIC Intro
Essential TOEIC &
Cabin Crew English

CONTENTS

품사 & 문장의 구조

품사란?

문장을 구성하는 각 단어는 의미meaning와 역할function에 따라 8가지 종류로 분류되며, 이를 "품사Part of Speech"라고 한다.

내용어 (Content Words)	문장의 내용을 결정하는 어휘	명사, 형용사, 부사, 동사
기능어 (Function Words)	내용어 사이에 들어가는 문법적 기능을 갖는 어휘	전치사, 접속사, 대명사, 관사

1 명사Noun - 이름의 모든 것

유형/무형의 사람, 동물, 장소, 사물 등을 지칭하는 어휘로서 문장 안에서 주어Subject, 목적어Object, 보어Complement의 역할을 한다.

* apple, book, sister, house : 보통명사
* coffee, air, sand, wisdom, beauty : 추상명사
* Tom, Seoul, the Han River : 고유명사

(1) 가산 명사: 셀 수 있는 명사
  - 사람: student, professor, customer, critic, applicant
  - 사물: facility, salary, bank, desk, building

(2) 불가산 명사: 셀 수 없는 명사
  - 추상명사: love, knowledge, success, hate, research
  - 물질명사: air, water, petrol, glass, money
  - 집합명사: baggage, furniture, stationary, equipment

2 대명사 Pronoun - 명사의 대타

사물이나 사람을 나타내는 명사를 다시 언급해주는데 사용되는 어휘로서, 문장 속에서 하는 역할에 따라 **주격, 목적격, 소유격**으로 변화한다.

	주격		목적격		소유격	
	단수	복수	단수	복수	단수	복수
1인칭	I	we	me	us	my	our
2인칭	you	you	you	you	your	your
3인칭	he/she/it	they	him/her/it	them	his/her/its	their

(1) 주격 인칭대명사: 주어자리에 옴

- <u>You</u> are very creative and <u>I</u> would like to recommend you for this position.
- <u>I</u> want to go aboad and stay there for a while.

(2) 소유격 인칭대명사: 명사 앞에서 소유관계를 나타냄

- Applicants should write down <u>their</u> name on the first page.

(3) 목적격 인칭대명사: 동사 혹은 전치사의 목적어 역할

- Visiting Mr. Smith is not a good choice for <u>us</u>.

(4) 소유대명사: 소유격+명사

- This is his car and that is <u>hers</u> her car.

3 동사Verb – 움직임을 보여주는 말

사람이나 사물의 상태나 동작을 나타내는 단어로서, 크게 be 동사와 일반 동사로 구분된다.

be 동사	"... 이다"라는 신분 혹은 "...에 있다"라는 존재를 나타낸다.	
일반 동사	자동사	목적어를 필요로 하지 않는 동사
	타동사	목적어를 필요로 하는 동사

(1) 자동사: 목적어(동사의 대상)가 필요 없음

- Susan will <u>stay</u> in Paris for a month.
- I am a cheerful and creative person.

(2) 타동사: 목적어(동사의 대상)가 필요함

- I <u>bought</u> a bunch of flowers for him.
- We should <u>raise</u> next year's production by 20 percent.

(3) 자동사+전치사 → 타동사처럼 목적어가 옴

respond to…	react to…	appeal to…
object to…	comply with…	participate in…
specialize in…	reside in…	look into…
deal with…	result from…	apologize for…

4 형용사Adjective – 명사를 수식하는 말

명사의 성질이나 상태를 설명하는 단어로서, 명사 앞에서 수식하거나 혹은 뒤에서 서술하는 경우로 나뉜다.

역할	명사수식	(ex) I met some nice students.
	주격보어 자리	(ex) They were cool.
	목적격보어 자리	(ex) The movie made me happy.

| 한정적 용법 | (ex) a **brown** shirt |
| 서술적 용법 | (ex) This **shirt** is brown. |

일반 형용사	성질 모습 상태 묘사	simple cheerful white accurate	간단한 명랑한 하얀 정확한
수량 형용사	수 혹은 양	each every all much many	각각 모든 모든 많은 양의 많은 갯수의
부정 형용사	정해지지 않은 것	some most all other	일부의 대부분의 모든 다른

5 부사Adverb - 꾸밈 말

부사는 형용사, 다른 부사, 혹은 동사를 앞에서 수식할 수 있고, 문장 전체를 수식하는 부사절도 있다.

동사 수식	(ex) He runs fast. (run 수식)
부사 수식	(ex) He runs very fast. (fast 수식)
형용사 수식	(ex) He is very smart. (smart 수식)
문장 수식	(ex) When he is tired, he drinks coffee.("he drinks coffee." 수식)

6 전치사 - 명사와 대명사가 쓰는 모자

전치사는 명사, 대명사, 혹은 동명사들 앞에 오는 어휘들과 연결되어 의미를 만든다. 장소, 방향, 시간, 이유 혹은 소유 등의 관계를 설명한다.

장소	at, on, in, in front of, opposite
방향	from, to, toward, out of

시간	at, on, during, until
이유	due to, because of
소유	of

7 접속사 - 연결시켜주는 말

접속사는 단어와 단어, 구와 구phrase: en 단어 이상의 의미 단위, 그리고 절과 절a clause: 주어와 동사가 들어 있는 의미 단위을 연결해준다.

단어 연결	(ex) bread and butter
구 연결	(ex) Would you like to dance or to sing?
절 연결	(ex) I love you but I can't marry with you.

8 관사Article와 감탄사Interjection - 명사 앞에 오는 말 & 감정 표현의 말

관사는 명사 앞에 오는 "a, an, the"를 말하며, 감탄사는 특별한 의미 없이 감정을 전달하기 위해 내는 소리를 뜻한다.

관사 활용 예시	He keeps a dog and a cat. The cat is bigger than the dog.
감탄사 예시	oh, oops, wow, bravo, well, etc

문장의 구조?

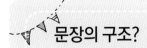

문장을 이루고 있는 요소

1 문장 구성의 핵심 요소: 주어, 동사, 목적어, 보어의 개념

주어	**동사의 주체** (한국어 "-은, -는, -이, -가"로 끝나는 단어) 명사, 대명사, to - 부정사, 동명사, 절 등이 주어가 될 수 있다. (1) 명사 주어: ex) Dogs usually bark at night. 　　　　　　　　ex) Sally is a school nurse. (2) 대명사 주어: ex) They want to visit us. (3) to - 부정사 주어: ex) To help other people is not easy. (4) 동명사 주어: ex) Eating healthy food is necessary. (5) 절 주어: ex) When we will arrive is not certain.
동사	주어의 동작이나 상태를 서술하는 어휘로, 조동사까지 포함된다. 동사는 주어가 단수 혹은 복수인가에 따라 변화한다.(한국어 "-하다, -이다"에 해당) ex) Tom is humorous. 　　They are really active. ex) Susan usually gets up early. 　　We get up at seven o'clock.
목적어	동사나 동사구의 대상이 되며, 명사, 대명사, to-부정사, 동명사, 절 등이 목적어가 될 수 있다. (1)　　주어　　동사　　목적어 　ex)　Jane　wants　a boy friend. 　　　 Jane　saw　　them. 　　　 Tom　wants　to play a computer game. 　　　 Tom　enjoys　playing a computer game. 　　　 They　think　that this is too expensive.

목적어	"-에게"가 따르는 간접목적어와 "-을, -를"이 따르는 직접목적어가 있으며 둘이 함께 사용될 때는 간접목적어가 먼저 위치한다. 간접목적어가 전치사와 연결되었을 때는 직접목적어가 먼저 온다. ex) My friend gave <u>me</u> <u>a book</u>. 　　　　　　　　간접목적어 직접목적어 　　　　　　　　<u>a book</u> to <u>me</u>. 　　　　　　　직접목적어　간접목적어 　　I will make <u>him</u> <u>a cake</u>. 　　　　　　　　간접목적어 직접목적어 　　　　　　<u>a cake</u> for <u>him.</u> 　　　　　직접목적어　간접목적어
보어	동사 혹은 동사구만으로는 부족한 경우에, 주어를 보충해주는 "주격 보어"와 목적어를 보충하는 "목적격 보어"가 있다. 　ex) Tom seems tired. (주격 보어) 　　　We thought him a liar. (목적격 보어)

2 구phrase와 절clause

(1) 구(phrase): 두 개 이상의 어휘가 모여 한 가지 품사 역할을 하는 의미 단위

　절(clause): 두 개 이상의 어휘가 모여 "주어 + 동사"관계가 형성된 것

① 명사구와 명사절: 명사처럼 주어, 목적어, 혹은 보어 역할

　　ex. **To learn a foreign language** is necessary. (명사구: 주어)

　　　It is necessary **to learn a foreign language**. (명사구: 보어)

　　　I know **that they will visit Seoul next week**. (명사절: 목적어)

② 형용사구와 형용사절: 명사를 수식하는 역할을 하며, 명사 뒤에서만 수식한다는 것이 형용사와 다름

　　ex. I need something **to eat in the train**. (형용사구)

　　　I need something **that I can eat in the train**. (형용사절)

③ 부사구와 부사절: 여러 단어가 모여 부사의 역할을 하는 것. 형용사, 다른 부사, 동사 혹은 절을 수식할

수 있음.

ex. They ate the lunch **in a hurry**. (동사 ate 수식)

English is not easy **to study**. (형용사 easy 수식)

I went to the meeting late **because I had to finish my work**. (부사절)

(2) 절(clause)의 종류: 등위절 / 종속절

① 등위절: and, but, or, so 등으로 대등한 관계로 연결되는 절

ex. **I like tea** but **she likes coffee**.

Could you clean the room and **could you set the table**?

② 종속절: 한 가지 품사의 역할을 하는 절로서, 명사절, 형용사절, 부사절 등이 있음.

a. 명사절: 관계대명사 what, 접속사 that, if, whether, 혹은 간접의문문의 의문사로 연결되고, 주어, 목적어

혹은 보어 역할

ex. She doesn't know **that Tom is the captain**.

What you believe is true.

Do they know **when the boss will arrive**?

b. 형용사절: 관계대명사와 관계부사로 연결되는 절로서, 선행사_{앞 문장에 있는 명사}를 수식하는 형용사 역할

ex. You should read **the book which tells about World War II**.

I remember **the day when I saw him at the library**.

c. 부사절: 특정한 접속사와 결합하여, 시간_{when, as, before, after...}, 조건_{if}, 이유 _{because, as...}, 양보_{although, even though}

등을 나타내며 부사 기능을 하는 절

ex. **When** you visit Seoul, feel free to contact me. (시간)

He is drinking cold water **because** he is very thirsty. (이유)

Although he is young, he is diligent. (양보)

If it snows tomorrow, we'll stay home. (조건)

Tip

완전자동사-보어가 필요 없는 동사

불완전자동사-보어가 필요한 동사

자동사-목적어가 필요 없는 동사

타동사-목적어가 필요한 동사

수여동사-간접목적어와 직접목적어가 필요한 동사

3 다섯 가지 문장 형식

문장은 **동사의 종류**에 따라 다섯 가지 형식으로 분류된다.

(1) 1형식: 주어+동사 [완전자동사]

ex. Career opportunities exist in many areas.
　　　주어　　　　동사　　　수식어

(2) 2형식: 주어+동사+주격보어 [불완전자동사]

ex. The products are expensive.
　　　주어　　　동사　　보어

(3) 3형식: 주어+동사+목적어 [완전타동사]

ex. The company earned two million dollars.
　　　주어　　　동사　　　목적어

(4) 4형식: 주어+동사+간접목적어+직접목적어 [수여동사]

ex. Tom lent me some money.
　　주어 동사 간목　직목

(5) 5형식: 주어+동사+목적어+목적보어 [불완전타동사]

ex. The residents keep their environment clean.
　　　주어　　　동사　　목적어　　　목적보어

🖐 Grammar Practice

01 Once Jane completes the application form, _____ will be sent to the HR for review.

   (A) it   (B) him   (C) itself   (D) them

02 The secretary _____ all the documents that were needed for the business meeting.

   (A) provided   (B) provision   (C) to provide   (D) providing

03 _____ of the survey data indicates that the new presidential election strategy will need considerable analysis.

   (A) Analyze   (B) Analyzed   (C) Analytical   (D) Analysis

04 Most of the candidates were fully qualified, but Linda's interview was very _____.

   (A) impressive   (B) impression   (C) impress   (D) impressively

05 For the investors, it is important _____ CV's new romantic film will be enthusiastically received or not.

   (A) where   (B) even   (C) whether   (D) owing to

06 Although this is a general _____, most teenagers are addicted to various computer games.

   (A) assumption   (B) assume   (C) assumptive   (D) assumed

07 The jazz festival has been postponed _____ unfavorable weather.

   (A) owing   (B) because of   (C) in spite of   (D) although

08 The CEO chose _____ Mr. Johnson for his outstanding service over the last 40 years.

(A) will honor   (B) to honor   (C) would honor   (D) honor

09 Please understand _____ we would prefer to be told a day in advance if you need to change the appointment.

(A) then   (B) that   (C) unlike   (D) instead of

10 The researchers found it _____ to solve them with the Azotec 736 software.

(A) ease   (B) eased   (C) easy   (D) easily

💡 Grammar Review TEST

01 _____ for the fifth arts contest of the National Art Museum must be received by May 1.

(A) Enter   (B) Entered   (C) Entering   (D) Entries

02 At the Christ Organization, _____ supplies to Africa has been the main topic since last year.

(A) donated   (B) donation   (C) donating   (D) donate

03 The managers agree that _____ deserves the credit for completing the two companies' deal.

(A) her   (B) she   (C) herself   (D) hers

04 GT, specializing in wireless communication equipment, _____ yesterday that it would start an online business.

(A) announcement   (B) announcing   (C) announced   (D) to announce

05 Your opinions are very important to us, so please _____ a customer satisfaction survey at the front desk.

(A) complete   (B) completion   (C) completely   (D) completed

06 Because _____ is necessary for customers to track the progress of their investment, JS Capital sends all of its clients monthly reports.

(A) there   (B) what   (C) that   (D) it

07 The chief editor of Europe Fashion magazine travels _____ to keep up with the trends of the world.

(A) extension   (B) extensively   (C) extensive   (D) extending

08 Samson's new line of dishwashers is _____ in price to its previous line, although the new designs are more attractive.

(A) comparable   (B) comparison   (C) comparably   (D) compare

09 If there are problems with your newly purchased products, you must contact the _____ directly for repair or replacement.

(A) distributor   (B) distribute   (C) distributive   (D) distributed

10 Please let _____ know at least a day in advance if you need to change your appointment.

(A) we   (B) us   (C) he   (D) they

필수어휘	의미 및 예문
1 object	① (동)동 ~에 반대하다 (to) He **object**ed to the label "Magician". ② (명) 사물
2 objection	(명) 반대
3 objective	① (형) 객관적인→(명) objectivity We need an **objective** and impartial report. ② (명) 목표 (= goal) Her main **objective** now is simply to stay in power.
4 comply	(동) (법, 명령) 따르다 (with) They **comply with** the rules.
5 compliant	(형) 순응하는, 따르는 They **are compliant with** the rules.
6 compliance	(명) 준수, 순응, 따름 They **are in compliant with** the rules.
7 rely depend	(동) 의지하다, 의존하다 (on) I **rely/depend on** my salary.
8 reliant dependent	(형) 의지하는, 의존하는 We are **reliant/dependent on** our parents.
9 reliable dependable	(형) 의지할 수 있는, 믿을 수 있는 He is a **reliable/dependable** friend.
10 contract	(동) 계약하다. Our company was **contract**ed to build shelters for the homeless. (명) 계약(서) They made a **contract** with the supplier.

필수어휘		의미 및 예문
11	subcontract	sub (=under)+contract: 계약 밑의 계약 → 하청계약
12	restore	(동) 복구하다, 복원하다 They want to **restore** the castle to its former glory.
13	imply	(동) 내포하다, 암시하다 Her statement **implies** a lack of confidence in the management of the company.
14	recommend	(동) 추천하다 I **recommend** the chicken in mushroom sauce.
15	involve	(동) 포함하다, 연관시키다 The job **involve**s traveling to Paris.
16	prevent	(동) 막다 (~from) His disability **prevents** him **from** driving.
17	specialize	(동) 전문으로 하다 (in) This restaurant **specializes** in seafood.
18	feature	(명) 특징 (동) 특징으로 삼다, 포함하다 This film **features** Hugh Grant as a driver.
19	replace	(동) re+place (다시+놓다→교체하다, 대체/대신하다) All the old desks need to be **replace**d.
20	secure	(형) 안전한, 확실한, 안심하는 (동) 확보하다, 고정시키다 He **secured** 1,000 votes. They **secured** the floorboards to the porch framing.

1. 효과적으로 음성을 만들기 위해서는 바른 자세가 필수적이다.

2. 정확한 발음으로 고객과 의사소통: 도착지, 편명, 비행시간, 지연사유 등 중요한 정보를 정확하게 전달한다.

3. 음성의 강약 조절: 단조롭게 외우듯 하지 않고 억양과 속도에 변화를 주어 다양하게 표현한다.

4. 안정감 있는 톤을 사용: 고객에게 안정감을 주고 설득력 있게 전달하기 위해 너무 높은 톤보다는 약간 낮은 톤을 사용한다.

5. 효과적으로 띄어 읽기: 띄어 읽기와 쉼표의 위치에 따라 문장의 의미가 변화하기 때문에 단어와 단어, 문장과 문장사이에 정확하게 띄어 읽는다.

6. 생동감 있고 부드러운 대화: 부자연스럽게 외운 문장을 전달하는 것이 아니라 승객과 편안하게 대화하듯이 방송한다.

비행절차에 따른 기내방송 안내표

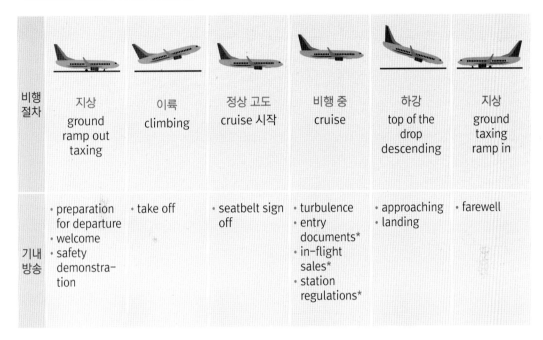

비행 절차	지상 ground ramp out taxing	이륙 climbing	정상 고도 cruise 시작	비행 중 cruise	하강 top of the drop descending	지상 ground taxing ramp in
기내 방송	• preparation for departure • welcome • safety demonstra- tion	• take off	• seatbelt sign off	• turbulence • entry documents* • in-flight sales* • station regulations*	• approaching • landing	• farewell

* 표시는 국제선에서만 방송함

CHAPTER
02

명사와 관사

명사란?
사람이나 사물의 이름을 나타내거나 추상적인 개념을 나타내는 품사

1 명사의 분류

(1) 가산명사(Count Noun) - **셀 수 있는 명사**. 단수일 때는 **부정관사나 정관사**, 복수일 때는 + (e)s

ex. table, chair, book, student, form, skill, course, job, party, system, office....

(2) 불가산명사(Non-count Noun) - **셀 수 없는 명사**. 단수 복수의 구분이 없이 **항상 단수 취급**.

ex. water, air, money, advice, knowledge, information, equipment, baggage, luggage...

(3) 복합명사 - 두 개 이상의 명사가 한 단어처럼 쓰이는 경우, 이러한 명사구를 일컬음

ex. account number / application form / communication skills / sales department / insurance coverage / job appraisal / safety procedure / retirement party / media coverage / heating system / customs office / savings account....

(4) 일반명사 / 사람 명사의 구분

engineering – engineer / attendance – attendant / application – applicant / consultation – consultant / authorization – author / contribution – contributor / performance – performer / occupation – occupant / translation – translator ....

Tip 한정사란? 명사 앞에 놓여서 명사의 의미를 한정해주는 표현

    a. 관사 – 부정관사(a/an), 정관사(the)
    b. 소유격 – 인칭대명사의 소유격 (my, your, his, her, their, our)
    c. 지시 대명사 – this, that (these, those)
    d. 수량 형용사 – many, much, few, a few, little, a little, a lot of....
    ☞ 관사, 소유격, 지시대명사, 수량형용사 뒤는 명사자리!
    ☞ 지시대명사, 소유격 대명사, 수량형용사가 한정사로 쓰이며 이들은 부정
      관사나 정관사와 함께 쓰일 수 없음!
      ex. 지시대명사: Print **this report**, please.
                            지시대명사 this가 명사 report를 수식 ("이")
      ex. 소유격 대명사: This is **my report**.
                             소유격 my가 명사 report를 수식 ("나의")
      ex. 수량형용사: I have written **many reports** this month.
                            형용사 many가 명사 report를 수식

2 명사의 역할 – 주어, 보어, 타동사의 목적어, 전치사의 목적어

(1) 주어: 동사 앞에서 행위의 주체를 나타내는 주어

    ex. **The president** rejected the proposal. (동사 rejected의 주어)

(2) 보어: 2형식에서는 주격보어 / 5형식에서는 목적격 보어

    ex. Tom is **a student**. (be 동사인 is의 주격보어 역할)

    ex. Everyone considered Tom **a genius**. (considered에 대한 목적격 보어)

(3) 타동사의 목적어: 타동사 뒤에서 행위의 대상을 나타내는 목적어

    ex. We usually eat **lunch**. (타동사 eat의 목적어)

(4) 전치사의 목적어: 전치사 뒤에서 전치사의 목적어

    ex. The building is under **construction**. (전치사 under의 목적어)

3 명사가 쓰이는 형태

(1) 형용사 + 명사

ex. The company needs **competitive applicants.**
　　　　　　　　　　　　形容詞　　　　名詞

(2) 소유격 + 명사

ex. **My supervisor** asked a contractor to submit the estimate.
　　소유격　명사

(3) 관사 (+ 부사 + 형용사) + 명사

ex. He carried **an umbrella** with him.
　　　　　　　관사　명사

ex. This is **a newly purchased computer.**
　　　　　　관사　부사　　형용사　　　명사

(4) 명사 + 명사 = 복합명사

ex. This milk has passed the **expiration date.**
　　　　　　　　　　　　　　명사　　명사

✅ 명사의 기능을 할 수 있는 대용어구

1. 대명사
2. 동명사 V + ing
3. 부정사 to + V
4. 명사절 … that 주어 + 동사..

---

① 대명사

The committee really like **her** as a new CEO.

The travel agent sent **them** an itinerary of Paris.

② 동명사

They <u>enjoy</u> **climbing** the mountain.

I <u>look forward to</u> **meeting** the new boss tomorrow.

③ 부정사

I <u>like</u> **to visit** my relatives on weekends.

Jane already <u>decided</u> **to purchase** a new car.

④ 명사절

I <u>believe</u> **that the new project will be successful.**

Our professor will <u>report</u> **whether the stress is related with students'satisfaction of the curriculum or not.**

Tip 명사자리

   ⓐ 관사 + 명사 – ex. I have **a book**.
   ⓑ 관사 + 형용사 + 명사 – ex. I have **an expensive book**.
   ⓒ 관사 + 지시대명사(수량형용사) + 명사 – I gave **that book** to him.
   ⓓ 소유격 + 명사 – ex. He likes **my book**.
   ⓔ 전치사 + 명사 – ex. He went **to a bookstore** to buy some books.
   ⓕ 타동사 + 명사 – ex. He **sent the book** back to me.
   ⓖ 구동사 + 명사 – ex. He **looked at the book** everyday.
   ⓗ 명사 + 전치사 – ex. Mark is the ideal **candidate for** the program
      manager position.
   ⓘ 복합명사 – ex. I'll need the **sales report** for a meeting on Monday.

01 Parents are advised to use _____ when they allow their kids under 6 to watch TV programs.

(A) cautious   (B) cautiously

(C) cautioned   (D) caution

02 Please visit our Web site to review the requirements before applying for a permit or _____.

(A) license   (B) licensor

(C) licensed   (D) licensing

03 He is unable to accept the invitation to the president's dinner party because of a scheduling _____.

(A) conflicts   (B) conflicting

(C) conflict   (D) conflicted

04 Our company has clearly been experiencing considerable growth in the online market, so it is seeking additional _____ in this field.

(A) assistant   (B) assist

(C) assisted   (D) assistance

05 As you know, all interoffice _____ will be delivered to each department's mail box.

(A) correspondent   (B) corresponds

(C) correspondence   (D) corresponding

06 With a 15 percent _____ in net profit over the last year, NB Trading Co. is clearly showing significant growth.

(A) increases

(B) to increase

(C) increase

(D) increased

07 The Sales Department still has several outstanding _____ related to the JJ project, whose profits have been decreasing continuously.

(A) expends

(B) expenses

(C) expended

(D) expensive

08 R & S has designed some modern _____ in the city hall.

(A) structure

(B) structures

(C) structural

(D) structurally

09 The purpose of this marketing is to attract consumers from _____ age groups.

(A) every

(B) a little

(C) much

(D) all

10 The office provided an _____ to the owner who wanted to change his office building to residential one.

(A) estimate

(B) estimates

(C) estimated

(D) estimating

01 A careful _____ of the consumer survey shows that customers are not willing to spend after the recent economic crisis.

(A) evaluative　　　　　　　　　　　　(B) evaluate

(C) evaluated　　　　　　　　　　　　(D) evaluation

02 The management of Good Neighbors hopes to increase the _____ of organ donators consistently.

(A) numerous　　　　　　　　　　　　(B) number

(C) numeral　　　　　　　　　　　　　(D) numbered

03 Lion Inc. announced its fourth-quarter _____ yesterday, which was much less than expected.

(A) profited　　　　　　　　　　　　　(B) profitable

(C) profitably　　　　　　　　　　　　(D) profit

04 Bank of America has employed a competent financial advisor to ensure a fair _____ of funds across all divisions.

(A) distribute　　　　　　　　　　　　(B) distribution

(C) distributional　　　　　　　　　　(D) distributed

05 By placing a heavy _____ on customer satisfaction, Macy's has built up a positive reputation in the area.

(A) emphatically　　　　　　　　　　(B) emphasis

(C) emphasize　　　　　　　　　　　(D) emphasized

06 Lucy Bakery doesn't offer _____ of cakes to locations outside Mexico City due to the increasing costs.

(A) delivery

(B) deliver

(C) delivered

(D) deliverable

07 Unlike its competitors, Nexon Tires has showed steady _____ in each quarter this year.

(A) grown

(B) growth

(C) grow

(D) grew

08 In _____ to your advertisement for a secretary, I have sent my resume and a letter of recommendation to your Personnel Department.

(A) respond

(B) response

(C) responsive

(D) responded

09 Because of Tom's excellent _____, the personnel manager contacted him to schedule an interview.

(A) qualifications

(B) qualify

(C) qualifies

(D) qualified

10 If you would like further information on the _____ session, please contact attorney Bob Johnson at 342-6398.

(A) to train

(B) was trained

(C) training

(D) trainable

	필수어휘	의미 및 예문
1	representative	(명) 대표(자), (판매) 직원 We'll increase our team of **representatives** to help meet sales targets.
2	grant	(동) 승인하다, 인정하다. She **grant**ed their request. Access to the European market will be **grant**ed.
3	anticipate	(동) 예상하다, 기대하다 We don't **anticipate** any trouble.
4	install	(동) 설치하다 The plumber is coming tomorrow to **install** the new washing machine.
5	acknowledge	(동) (사실로) 인정하다 She **acknowledged** that she had been at fault.
6	exceed	(동) 넘다, 초과하다 The final cost should not **exceed** $5,000.
7	excess	(명) exceed의 명사→과도, 과잉, 초과액 They both eat to **excess** (=too much).
	access	cf) access: 접근 (to) The only **access** to the village is by boat.
8	address	(명) 주소 (동) 연설하다, (문제) 고심하다 We'll **address** that question at the next meeting.
9	implement	(동) 이행/수행하다 The country had been slow to **implement** the new European directive. cf) implementation: (명) 이행, 수행
10	conduct	(동) (특정활동) 하다 (a survey, an experiment, an inquiry, etc.) We're **conduc**ting a survey to find out what our customers think of their local bus service.
11	submit	(동) 제출하다 You must **submit** your application before 1 January. cf) turn in; hand in
12	attend	(동) 참석하다 You are invited to **attend** our annual wine-tasting evening.

	필수어휘	의미 및 예문
13	participate	(동) 참가/참여하다 (in) They didn't **participate** in the session.
14	respond	(동) 응답하다 (to) She never **respond**ed to my letter.
	reply	(동) 대답하다, 응하다 (to) He never **repli**ed to any of my letters.
15	receipt	(명) 수취, 받음 I'm calling to acknowledge **receipt** of the letter.
	a receipt	(명) 영수증 Can I have a **receipt**?
16	stand out	(동) 두드러지다 The black lettering really **stands out** on that orange background.
	outstanding	(형) 뛰어난 The region is renowned for its **outstanding** natural beauty.
17	reimburse	(동) (돈을) 갚다: 다른 사람 혹은 단체를 위해 자비를 쓴 경우 그에 상응하는 돈을 되 돌려주는 것 The company is going to **reimburse** me for the business trip.
18	go up rise increase	(동) 상승하다, 오르다 The cost of the project has **increase**d significantly. cf) significantly/dramatically/sharply: 　상당히 　steadily: 꾸준하게 　slightly/a little/a bit: 약간 위의 부사를 활용하여 증가폭을 표현할 수 있다.
	skyrocket soar	(동) 급등하다 Housing prices have **skyrocket**ed in recent months.
19	go down fall decrease	(동) 하락하다, 떨어지다 Our market share has **decrease**d sharply. cf) significantly/dramatically/sharply: 　상당히 　steadily: 꾸준하게 　slightly/a little/a bit: 약간 위의 부사를 활용하여 증가폭을 표현할 수 있다.
	plunge plummet	(동) 급락하다 Our income has **plunge**d dramatically.
20	notify inform	(동) 누군가에게 무엇인가를 알려주다 (발표내용과 발표를 듣는 대상이 나와야 한다) Please **notify us** of **any change of address**. We are pleased to **inform you that your application has been accepted**.
	announce state declare	(동) 알리다, 발표하다 (발표내용만 나오고 듣는 대상은 필요하지 않다) The president has **announce**d that public spending will be increased next year.

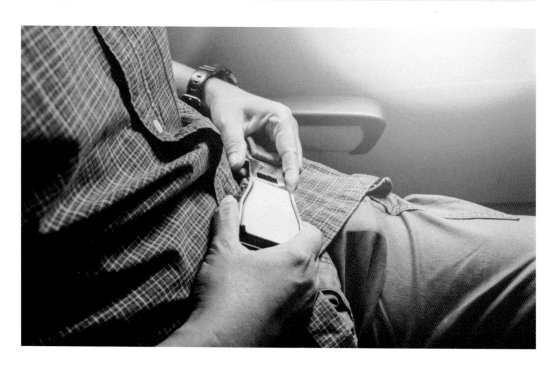

손님 여러분, 도시명까지 가는 대한항공 KE102편, 잠시 후약 30분 후에 출발하겠습니다. 갖고 계신 짐은 앞 좌석 아래나 선반 속에 보관해주시고, 지정된 자리에 앉아 좌석벨트를 매 주시기 바랍니다. 감사합니다.

Ladies and gentlemen,

This is Korean Air flight ____ bound for ____ (via ____). We are just (a few/ ____) minutes away from departure.

Please make sure that your carry-on items are stored in the overhead bins or under the seat in front of you.

Also, please take your assigned seat and fasten your seat belt. Thank you.

Airline TOEIC Intro
Essential TOEIC &
Cabin Crew English

CHAPTER
03

대명사

대명사란?

앞에 쓴 명사의 반복을 피하기 위해 해당 명사를 대신해서 쓰는 말

ex. 나는 남주혁을 좋아합니다. <u>그</u>는 연기력도 좋고 선한 사람입니다.

대명사 = 남 주 혁

앞에 쓴 명사의 반복을 피하기 위해 해당 명사를 대신해서 쓰는 말

대명사의 종류 – 인칭대명사 / 지시대명사 / 부정대명사로 분류될 수 있음

---

1 인칭대명사

'그', '그녀', '당신'처럼 사람을 가리키는 대명사로 인칭, 성, 수, 격에 따라 형태가 달라진다.

		주격	소유격	목적격	소유대명사	재귀대명사
1인칭	단수(나)	I	my	me	mine	myself
	복수(우리)	we	our	us	ours	ourselves
2인칭	단수(당신)	you	your	you	yours	yourself
	복수(당신들)	you	your	you	yours	yourselves
3인칭	남성(그)	he	his	him	his	himself
단수	여성(그녀)	she	her	her	her	herself
	사물(그것)	it	its	it	–	itself
복수(그들,그것들)		they	their	them	theirs	themselves

(1) 인칭대명사의 주격은 주어자리, 목적격은 목적어 자리, 소유격은 명사 앞에 온다.

ex. The landlord of **our** <u>apartment</u> showed **us** the bathroom.

ex. Dr. Kuster was satisfied with **his** <u>life</u> in Korea.

(2) 소유대명사는(~의 것) 주어, 목적어, 보어 자리에 온다.

> ex. **My car** has two doors. **Hers** has four. – 주어
>
> ex. The judge likes **my idea**. She dislikes **theirs**. – 목적어

(3) 재귀대명사는 주어와 목적어가 같은 대상일 때 목적어 자리에 온다. 주어나 목적어를 강조하기 위해 쓸 때는 생략 가능하다. 때로는 전치사 by 등과 어울려 특정표현을 나타낸다.

> ex. Ming introduced **herself** to a new classmate. – 주어=목적어
>
> ex. **We ourselves** should get a shot against influenza. – 주어 강조
>
> ex. He have put a lot of work into making a table **by himself**. – 그 혼자서

2 지시대명사

'이것', '저것'과 같이 대상을 가리킬 때 쓰는 대명사

this / these	이것, 이 사람 / 이것들, 이 사람들
that / those	저것, 저 사람 / 저것들, 저 사람들

(1) 지시대명사 that과 those는 비교 대상이 되는 명사의 반복을 피하기 위해 쓴다.

> ex. Our **price** is lower than **that** of other shopping malls.
>
> ex. This month's **reports** are better than **those** of last month.

(2) 지시대명사는 명사 앞에 온다. this/that은 단수 명사 앞, these/those는 복수명사 앞에!

> ex. **This** laundry machine is under warranty.
>
> ex. **Those** chairs are well-designed items.

3 부정대명사

'어떤 사람', '어떤 것'처럼 정확한 수나 양을 알 수 없어서 막연하게 말할 때 쓰는 대명사이다. 부정대명사의 부정은 '아니다'의 뜻이 아니라 '정확히 정할 수 없다'의 뜻이다. 또한 뒤에 나온 명사를 수식하는 부정형용사로도 쓰인다.

all	모든 것, 모든 사람	each	각각
both	둘 다	some	어떤 것, 어떤 사람들

(1) some과 any는 모두 몇몇, 약간의 뜻으로 쓰이지만, some은 긍정문에 any는 부정문, 의문문, 조건문에 쓰인다.

    ex. This calculator has **some** problems.

    ex. I have not seen **any** of these movies.

(2) 사람이나 사물이 둘이 있을 경우 그 중 하나는 one, 나머지 하나는 the other로 나타낸다.

    ex. I bought two books. **One** is an essay; **the other** is a magazine.

사람이나 사물이 셋 이상 있을 경우 그 중 하나는 one, 또 다른 하나는 another, 그 중 다른 몇 개는 others, 나머지 전부는 the others로 나타낸다.

    ex. The company has many branches. **One** is in New Yok, **another** is in Paris and **others** are in London.

    ex. Linda has five different colors' jackets. **One** is black, **another** is white and **the others** are blue.

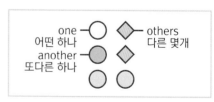

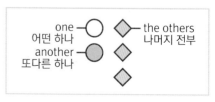

🖐 Grammar Practice

01 Company representatives spend the whole week answering _____ phones and e-mails.

(A) its　　　　　　　　　　　　　　(B) her

(C) our　　　　　　　　　　　　　　(D) their

02 Eco & Co. did not have _____ management skills to survive in the Asian cosmetic market.

(A) another　　　　　　　　　　　　(B) some

(C) any　　　　　　　　　　　　　　(D) few

03 For _____ with dietary restrictions, Air Canada provides special in - flight meals if you request in advance.

(A) those　　　　　　　　　　　　　(B) them

(C) whose　　　　　　　　　　　　　(D) which

04 If you receive any questions about next year's budge, please send _____ to the Accounting Department.

(A) they　　　　　　　　　　　　　(B) their

(C) them　　　　　　　　　　　　　(D) theirs

05 Jolly's has been voted the best Italian restaurant in San Francisco for three consecutive years, and its chef has been awarded for _____ unique recipes.

(A) himself　　　　　　　　　　　　(B) his

(C) him　　　　　　　　　　　　　　(D) he

06 Mr. Lee reviewed the business plan by _____ over the weekend to meet the deadline for the proposal.

(A) he   (B) him

(C) himself   (D) his own

07 Food processing factories in Ohio regions are working at full capacity to handle the demand for _____ corn products.

(A) they   (B) their

(C) themselves   (D) theirs

08 Amy is planning _____ business trip to the 2020 Fall/Winter Collections at Paris, London, and Milan.

(A) she   (B) her

(C) hers   (D) herself

09 _____ who have worked more than three years in the International Trade Department are eligible for this position.

(A) Them   (B) Their

(C) That   (D) Those

10 If _____ arrives at the airport late, Lisa will miss her flight to London.

(A) Lisa   (B) she

(C) her   (D) they

Grammar Review TEST

01 After Jane reviewed the CEO's travel reimbursement requests, _____ sent an e-mail to him.

(A) her
(B) she
(C) hers
(D) herself

02 If you receive the packages from Toy World, please send _____ to Mr. Jang in the Sales Department.

(A) they
(B) their
(C) them
(D) theirs

03 The marketing director will have a meeting with the advertising copywriter of Star Ad. to share new promotion ideas with _____.

(A) he
(B) him
(C) himself
(D) his

04 All registered participants in the Seoul City Marathon for Breast Cancer Care will receive a T-shirt printed with _____ logo.

(A) it
(B) its
(C) their
(D) they

05 If the medicine has expired, you should take _____ to the pharmacy for disposal.

(A) one
(B) it
(C) them
(D) some

06 George has shown _____ to be a skilled negotiator by solving the conflicts between the landlord and the tenants.

(A) he

(B) him

(C) himself

(D) his

07 Maria had to arrive early at the office to prepare for staff meeting _____, while the rest of her team came later.

(A) her

(B) herself

(C) her own

(D) hers

08 According to the weather forecast, today will be severly rainy, but we forgot to bring an umbrella with _____.

(A) me

(B) you

(C) us

(D) them

09 JBC Broadcasting offers several staff workshops and encourages its employees to be responsible for _____ training schedules.

(A) they

(B) them

(C) themselves

(D) their own

10 Invitation letters to the charity party were sent to all 30 local representatives, but _____ will be able to attend.

(A) little

(B) few

(C) whoever

(D) so

TOEIC ESSENTIAL VOCA

필수어휘	의미 및 예문
1 equipment	(명) 장비 All of the medical **equipment** must be sterilized before use.
2 on schedule	(부) 예정대로 The materials did not arrive **on schedule**.
3 complimentary	① (형) 무료의 As theater employees, we get **complimentary** tickets. ② (형) 칭찬하는 She wasn't very **complimentary** about your performance, was she?
4 complementary	(형) 상호보완전인 The **complementary** skills among the three executives created an effective leadership team.
5 reduce	(동) 줄이다, 감소시키다 Do nuclear weapons really **reduce** the risk of war?
6 attract	(동) 유인하다, 매료시키다 The circus is **attract**ing huge crowds.
7 file	(동) 문서를 보관하다, 소송하다 We **file** these reports under country of origin. The police **file**d charges against the two suspects.
8 postpone	(동) 연기하다 (=delay; put off) They decided to **postpone** their holiday until next year.
9 forward	(동) (누군가에게 무언가를) 보내다, 전송하다 I'll **forward** his email to you if you're interested.
10 fund	(명) 자금, 기금. It'll be a challenge to raise campaign **fund**s for the election. (동) 자금을 대다 The company has agreed to **fund** my trip to Japan.

	필수어휘	의미 및 예문
11	refund	(동) re+fund (다시+자금화하다) 환불하다 The office **refund**ed my expenses.
12	permit	① (동) 허락하다, 허가하다 The regulations do not **permit** much flexibility. ② (명) 허가서 (**a permit**) She has managed to obtain **a** temporary residence **permit**.
13	indicate	(동) (사실) 나타내다, 명시하다 She **indicate**d to me that she didn't want me to say anything.
14	obligate	(동) 의무를 지우다, 강요하다 The store is not **obligate**d to replace the product.
15	expire	(동) 만료되다, 만기되다 My passport **expire**s next month.
16	confidential	(형) 비밀의 A person's medical records are **confidential**.
17	confident	(형) 자신감 있는, 자신만만한 Are you **confident** that enough people will attend the event?
18	flexible	(형) 유연한, 융통성 있는 My schedule is **flexible** – I could arrange to meet with you any day next week.
19	eligible	(형) 적격의, 자격이 있는 (for) Is he **eligible** for the incentive?
20	mandatory	(형) 의무적인, 법에 정해진 The test includes a **mandatory** essay question.

🎙️ 기내방송 환영인사 WELCOME: GENERAL (국제선)

여러분, 안녕하십니까.[인사]

스카이팀 회원사인 저희 대한항공은 여러분의 탑승을 진심으로 환영합니다.

이 비행기는 나리타를 거쳐 도쿄까지 가는 대한항공701편입니다.

[공동운항] 저희 대한항공은 일본항공과 공동 운항 하고 있습니다.

목적지_{중간도착지}인 도쿄까지 예정된 비행시간은 이륙 후 2시간0분입니다.

오늘 _{성명}기장을 비롯한 저희 승무원들은 여러분을 정성껏 모시겠습니다.

[기내판매 전담승무원 탑승시]
또한 이 구간은 비행시간이 짧은 관계로 구입을 원하시는 면세품을 미리 주문 받고 있습니다. 이륙 후 기내판매 담당 승무원에게 말씀해주시면 식사서비스가 끝난 후 전달해 드리겠습니다.

출발을 위해 좌석벨트를 매주시고 등받이와 테이블을 제자리로 해주십시오.

그리고 휴대전화와 전자기기는 비행기 항법장비에 영향을 줄 수 있으니 전원을 꺼 주시기 바랍니다.

계속해서 기내 안전에 관해 안내해 드리겠습니다.

잠시 화면/승무원을 주목해주시기 바랍니다.

Good morning /afternoon/evening, ladies and gentlemen.

Captain Family Name and the entire crew would like to welcome you on board Korean Air, a SkyTeam member.

This is flight 701 bound for Tokyo (via_____).

[공동운항] code-sharing with Japan (Airlines)

Our flight time today will be 2hours and 10 minutes after take-off.

현지 승무원 탑승시	[일반적인 경우] We have (A) Japan based cabin crew on board.

During the flight, our cabin crew will be happy to serve you in any way we can.

To prepare for departure, please fasten your seat belt and return your seat and tray table to the upright position.

We also ask you to turn off all mobile phones as they can interfere with the aircraft's navigational system.

And please direct your attention for a few minutes to the video screens /or a cabin crew for safety information.

Airline TOEIC Intro
Essential TOEIC &
Cabin Crew English

CHAPTER 04

동사

동사란?

문장의 핵심이 되는 동사는 대략 5가지 형태로 구분된다. 기본형 / 3인칭 단수형 / 과거형 / 현재분사형 / 과거분사형으로 나누어 학습하면 효과적이다.

#동사의 종류를 크게 자동사와 타동사로 구분하여 이해할 수 있다.

1 자동사

목적어 필요 없음: 자동사 + 전치사 + 목적어전치사에 대한 목적어가 기본형태

    ex. John <u>swims</u> in the pond.

        She <u>walks</u> slow.

        They <u>live</u> in Canada.

        I <u>laughed at</u> the scene.

        Jane <u>listened to</u> me.

2 타동사

목적어 필요목적어는 직접목적어와 간접목적어가 있음

    ex. I usually <u>drink</u> <u>milk</u> in the morning.
             타동사   목적어

        Susan told <u>me</u> good <u>news</u>.
                간접목적어   직접목적어

3 연결동사

목적어가 필요 없는 자동사로서, be, taste, seem, like 또는 look은 동사부류로서 감각, 존재 등을 나타내는 동사이다. 연결동사 뒤에 형용사 혹은 주격보어가 온다.

ex. She <u>is</u> smart.

You <u>look</u> tired today.

This coffee <u>tastes</u> good.

Tom <u>became</u> a steward last year.

Tip 주의해야 할 동사 부류

타동사	access / accompany / alert / appreciate / approach / attend / approve / consult / contact / disclose / discuss / enhance / exceed / facilitate / implement / inspect / marry / mention / notify / overcome / reach / regret / resemble / visit	ex. I will marry Susie. They must discuss the issue. He always attends staff meetings.
자동사	add to, agree with(on/to), apologize to, complain about, deal with. depend on, graduate from, head toward, interfere with, look for, major in, proceed with, react to, refrain from, respond to, share with, succeed in, sympathize with, wait for, consent to	ex. They complained of new curriculum. Don't wait for me. The team experimented with brown rice.

4 사역동사

문장의 주체가 스스로 행하지 않고 남_{목적어}에게 그 행동이나 동작을 하게 하는 동사

주어 + make, have, help, let + 목적어 + 동사 원형	ex. He **made** me **stay** longer. I will **help** you **move** the sofa.
주어 +allow, cause, force, get + 목적어 + to 동사	ex. The storm **caused** us **to cancel** the picnic. You **got** me **to study** for the test. He **allowed** her **to leave** early.
have, get + 목적어 + p.p.(과거분사형)	ex. I **had** my car **fixed** at the garage. She **got** the wall **painted** in blue.

하나, 4형식으로 착각하기 쉬운 3형식 동사 유의!

• suggest, propose, introduce, announce, explain, mention, indicate, describe, prove

ex. It is my pleasure to **introduce to you** the world-renowned singer-song writer PSY.

둘, 목적보어로 명사, 형용사, 원형부정사, to 부정사가 옴

• The noise outside **made** our lecture **impossible**.

Grammar Practice

01 The TX Train _____ a dramatically fast way for residents to commute to the city.

(A) to provide   (B) providing   (C) provides   (D) provide

02 Our company had to _____ some of urgent items from a domestic market as the shipment had been delayed for a few weeks.

(A) be purchased   (B) have purchased

(C) being purchased   (D) purchase

03. Please remember that the 15 percent discount for newly registered customers _____ only to online orders.

(A) apply   (B) applying   (C) applies   (D) application

04 Because of the heavy rain, the World Class Baseball game _____ unfortunately last night.

(A) have been cancelled   (B) has been cancelled

(C) cancelled   (D) was cancelled

05 Singapore Lion Hotel' spokesperson _____ a press conference about the merger with J. W. Groups.

(A) is held   (B) hold   (C) will hold   (D) has been hold

06 Five years ago Dr. Miller _____ Angels Medical School to start his own clinic in downtown.

(A) leave   (B) left   (C) will leave   (D) was left

07 Additional materials must be _____ by Friday for the Senior Town construction project to be completed on schedule.

(A) to order   (B) order   (C) ordered   (D) orders

08 Please complete a survey form at the front desk so we can _____ this workshop better meet your needs.

(A) make   (B) have made

(C) making   (D) made

09 Dr. James _____ World History at University of North Carolina a few years ago and will give the same lecture again next semester.

(A) teach   (B) will teach

(C) had taught   (D) taught

10 Those wishing to participate in the workshop are _____ to register for it promptly because the seating is limited.

(A) suppose   (B) supposed

(C) to suppose   (D) supposing

Grammar Review TEST

01 Until Flex'Swimming Pool has been _____, using the pool is prohibited by the maintenance.

(A) renovate

(B) to renovate

(C) renovating

(D) renovated

02 The new president of the election _____ promptly at 12 o'clock tonight.

(A) announce

(B) is announced

(C) will be announced

(D) was announced

03 SS new line of computers are going to offer _____ with state-of-the-art software.

(A) us

(B) she

(C) they

(D) we

04 Our company always _____ a motivated and sincere candidate to join our organization.

(A) to seek

(B) seek

(C) seeks

(D) seeking

05 Of the 50 applicants, only 20 _____ a chance to attend interviews with the HR manager yesterday.

(A) have

(B) had

(C) has

(D) to have

06 The board of directors will _____ the seminar on recruiting new staff right after the annual meeting.

(A) start (B) starts

(C) started (D) starting

07 As a precaution, the laboratory _____ a new set of safety rules for all employees to obey.

(A) implement (B) implementation

(C) implements (D) implementing

08 Tiger & Co. has _____ essential office supplies to our office since 2007.

(A) provide (B) provided

(C) providing (D) to provide

09 Toff's cafe is _____ to announce the relocation to 5th Avenue in New York.

(A) to please (B) please

(C) pleased (D) have pleased

10 After a consultation with the labor yesterday, the CEO _____ it hard to reach an compromise.

(A) find (B) to find

(C) found (D) have found

	필수어휘	의미 및 예문
1	exclusive	(형) 배타적인→독점적인 This room is for the **exclusive** use of guests.
2	inclusive	(형) 포함된→포괄적인. The rent is **inclusive** of water and heating. The governments want to reach a settlement that is as **inclusive** as possible.
3	notable	(형) 주목할 만한, 유명한 Getting both sides to agree was a **notable** achievement.
4	substantial	(형) (크기, 중요성이) 상당한 She inherited a **substantial** fortune from her grandmother..
5	considerable	(형) 상당한 Damage to the house was **considerable**.
6	considerate	(형) 신중한, 사려깊은, 친절한 He is always polite and **considerate** toward his clients.
7	initial	(형) 처음의 My **initial** reaction was to laugh out loud.
8.	valid	(형) 유효한, 타당한 My passport is **valid** for another two years.
9	shipment	(명) 선적, 배송 A **shipment** of urgent medical supplies is expected to arrive very soon.
10	candidate	(명) 후보자, 지원자 (=applicant) How many **candidate**s are there for the job?.
11	regarding	(전) ~에 관한 (=about) The company is being questioned **regarding** its employment policy.
12	hold	(동) 쥐다, (행사를) 개최하다 The election will be **held** on 8 August.
13	accompany	(동) 동반하다, 동행하다 The course books are **accompanied** by two CDs. cf) company=cum+pane (같이+빵 먹다) 우리말에 '식구(食口)'가 '밥을 같이 먹는 사람들'이란 뜻인 것처럼 "company"도 '빵(pane)을 같이(cum) 먹는 집단'이란 뜻으로 '일행', '친구' 더 확대 되어서 '회사' 나 '사회'라는 의미로도 사용될 수 있다.

	필수어휘	의미 및 예문
14	apply	① (동) 적용하다 (A to B) They **applied** the new technology to farming. ② (동) 신청하다, 지원하다 (for) I've **applied** for a new job with the local newspaper.
15	application	(명) 적용, 지원, 지원서류 I've sent off **application**s for four jobs.
16	applicant	(명) 지원자 (=candidate) Many **applicant**s simply don't meet hiring requirements..
17	reimburse	(동) (돈을) 갚다: 다른 사람 혹은 단체를 위해 자비를 쓴 경우 그에 상응하는 돈을 되 돌려주는 것 The company is going to **reimburse** me for the business trip.
18	launch	(동) 발사하다, 시작하다 The program was **launch**ed a year ago.
19	renew	(동) re+new (다시+새롭게하다) → 재개하다, 갱신하다 I forgot to **renew** my season ticket.

20 **시제를 결정짓는 부사구들**

	과거	현재	미래

단순	1. yesterday
	2. last + 시간
	3. 시간 + ago
	4. in 과거연도
	5. recently
	6. once +
	7. those days
	8. as of + 과거시간
	   effective (~시간 부로)
	   starting
	   beginning
		1. 빈도부사
		   always
		   usually
		   freqently, often,
		   sometimes, occasionally
		2. every+시간
		3. 횟수(once, twice)+시간
		4. regularly, routinely
		   generally
			1. tomorrow
			2. this(coming)+시간
			3. next+시간
			4. in+미래연도
			5. soon/shortly
			6. in the future
			7. as of + 미래시간
			   effective (~시간 부로)
			   starting
			   beginning

진행		1. at the moment 2. currently, presently 3. (right) now	
완료	1. by the time+과거	1. just, already 2. yet 3. recently, lately 4. ever, never, before 5. since, for, so far, until now 6. for the last+시간 over past	1. by the time+현재(미래 대신)

손님 여러분, 방금 좌석벨트 표시등이 꺼졌습니다.

그러나 비행기가 갑자기 흔들리는 경우에 대비해 자리에서는 항상 좌석벨트를 매고 계시기 바랍니다.

그리고 선반을 여실 때는 안에 있는 물건이 떨어지지 않도록 조심해 주십시오.

손님 여러분께 다양한 혜택을 드리는 대한항공의 스카이 패스에 대한 정보는 기내지 모닝캄을 참고해주시고, 회원 가입을 원하시는 분은 저희 승무원에게 말씀해 주시기 바랍니다.

Ladies and gentlemen,

The captain has turned off the seatbelt sign.

In case of any unexpected turbulence, we strongly recommend you keep your seatbelt fastened at all times while seated. Please use caution when opening the overhead bins as the contents may fall out.

Please refer to the Morning Calm magazine in your seat pocket for information about SKYPASS membership. If you wish to join, please ask our cabin crew.

Airline TOEIC Intro
Essential TOEIC &
Cabin Crew English

CHAPTER

05

수일치

수일치란?

A dog dances. VS Dogs dance.

영어는 수에 민감한 언어이며, 주어가 단수 혹은 복수인가에 따라 동사의 변화가 있다. 주어가 단수인 A dog 일 때는 동사도 단수인 dances를, 주어가 복수인 Dogs 일 때는 동사도 복수인 dance를 사용한다.

1 수일치의 활용

주어에 따라 동사의 수를 일치시키는 것을 "수일치"라고 한다.
주어가 "가산명사셀 수 있는 명사"혹은 "불가산명사셀 수 없는 명사"인 가를 주목해야 한다.

(1) 단수 가산명사 일 때는 단수동사가 와야 함

　　ex. The University **intends** to establish a local campus.

(2) 불가산명사는 단수주어로 취급되어 뒤에 단수동사가 와야 함

　　ex. This furniture **arrives** fully assembled.

(3) to부정사와 동명사, 명사절은 단수동사로 받음

　　ex. To express your own opinion **is** known internationally for its strong business administration
　　　　program.

2 수일치와 함께 쓰는 어휘 파악

(1) 단수동사와 복수동사를 쓰는 수량 표현!

☞ 단수동사를 이끄는 표현: each / every / the number of / many a/ one of

☞ 복수동사를 이끄는 표현: all / some / many / a number of / several / a few

　　ex. **Every** citizen **pays** income taxes.

　　ex. **A number of** employees **have** recently been transferred to the new branch office.

(2)

most / all / some	+ of + the +	단수명사 – 단수동사
half / the rest	+ of + the +	복수명사 – 복수동사

　　ex. Most of the **seminar was** for new employees.

Grammar Practice

01 Pacific Electronics always _____ to expand its home appliance business into the European region.

(A) plan　　　　　(B) plans　　　　　(C) planning　　　　　(D) planned

02 According to the survey, television advertisements do not necessarily _____ sales.

(A) boosts　　　　(B) to boost　　　　(C) boost　　　　(D) boosted

03 If you _____ a lab top computer by the end of this month, you will get a special service with the warranty of 2 years.

(A) purchase   (B) has purchased   (C) purchases   (D) purchasing

04 All employees are _____ to complete travel expense reports immediately after returning from a business trip.

(A) require   (B) requires   (C) required   (D) requirement

05 Many of a newly selected books _____ usually displayed at the first raw of bookshelves.

(A) are   (B) is   (C) was   (D) were

06 Buffalo Whole-food Flee Market _____ you to purchase fresh organic products every weekend.

(A) allowance   (B) allows   (C) allowing   (D) allowable

07 Employees at our office should notify the manager in advance if they _____ to be absent for more than two days.

(A) expect   (B) expects   (C) expecting   (D) expected

08 My doctor suggests the patient that she _____ a sleeping pill before she goes to bed once a day.

(A) take   (B) takes   (C) to take   (D) taking

09 Using dried herbs as common salt and pepper will considerably _____ the taste of your home cooking recipes.

(A) effect   (B) effects   (C) affect   (D) affecting

10 A number of specialists _____ to be hired to operate and repair all the devices in this lab last year.

(A) has   (B) had   (C) have   (D) to have

💡 Grammar Review TEST

01 Alice Kitchen is _____ to announce the opening of its third branch on 6th Street in Chicago.

(A) please   (B) pleases   (C) pleasure   (D) pleased

02 Louis Cosmetics will _____ a variety of anti-aging creams to achieve high profit objectives.

(A) launch   (B) launching   (C) to launch   (D) launched

03 The current life style trends _____ the fast change of home appliances.

(A) indicate   (B) indicates   (C) indicating   (D) has indicated

04 A 20% discount _____ to all purchases over $50 as Outdoor Activities Apparel is eager to promote its new line of climbing outfits.

(A) apply   (B) applying   (C) applies   (C) application

05 Bobby's Cosmetics started 30 years ago as a small business that _____ on using only the best ingredients in its products.

(A) insist   (B) insisting   (C) insistent   (D) insisted

06 Ms. Ellis, the general manager's secretary, _____ office supplies every Thursday, so please let her know what you need by Wednesday.

(A) order
(B) orders

(C) ordering
(D) orderable

07 Each of the new employees _____ a guide line that provides information about company regulations.

(A) receive
(B) receives

(C) receiving
(D) receipt

08 While the railway tracks are closed to repair the damage from the heavy rain, the trains _____ temporarily.

(A) will be suspended
(B) suspends

(C) suspending
(D) to suspend

09 J&B co. better _____ our business needs, although its shipments take a little longer than other suppliers.

(A) to meet
(B) meets

(C) meet
(D) meeting

10 Mr. Cooper has asked that we _____ the potential risks more carefully before deciding to invest in the property market.

(A) considering
(B) consider

(C) are considered
(D) are considering

	필수어휘	의미 및 예문
1	fund-raiser	(명) 모금 행사, 모금담당자 She was a campaign **fundraiser** for two former Presidents..
2	merchandise	(명) 상품 Shoppers complained about poor quality **merchandise** and high prices.
3	consent	(명) 동의 (=agreement/permission) They can't publish your name without your **consent**.
4	expert	(명) 전문가 (=professional) He is an **expert** on 15th-century Italian art.
5	expertise	(명) 전문적 지식 She has considerable **expertise** in French history.
6	pollute	(동) 오염시키다 We won't invest in any companies that **pollute** the environment.
7	pollution pollutant	(명) 오염, 오염물질(셀 수 없는 명사) The beach was covered with **pollution**. (명) 오염물질 (셀 수 있는 명사) Pesticide is a harmful **pollutant** to the environment.
8	acquisition	(명) 획득, 인수 The museum's latest **acquisition** is a four-million-dollar sculpture.
9	liability liable	(명) 책임, 의무 (=responsibility) He denies any **liability** for the damaged caused. (형) 책임이 있는 (=responsible) You will be **liable** for any damage caused.
10	qualification qualified	(명) 자격, 자격증 You'll never get a good job if you don't have any **qualification**s. (형) 자격을 갖춘, 적격의 What makes you think that you are **qualified** for this job?
11	itinerary	(명) 여행일정표 The tour operator will arrange transport and plan your **itinerary**.

	필수어휘	의미 및 예문
12	vary	(동) (크기, 모양) 서로 다르다 The samples **varied** in quality but were generally acceptable.
	various	(형) 다양한 The author gave **various** reasons for having written the book.
	variety	(명) 여러 가지 다양함, 다양성 Work on the production line is monotonous and lacks **variety**. cf) a variety of=various
13	diverse	(형) 다양한 New York is a very culturally **diverse** city.
	diversity	(명) 다양성 Does TV adequately reflect the ethnic and cultural **diversity** of the country?
	diversify	(동) 다양화하다 You should be careful to **diversify** the production line. cf) diversification: 다양화
14	extend	(동) (길이, 기간) 늘이다 I need to **extend** my visa. cf) extension: (전화) 내선, 내선번호
15	expand	(동) (부피) 넓히다, 팽창하다 We've **expanded** the business by opening two more overseas branches.
16	adopt	(동) 채택하다, 입양하다 I think it's time to **adopt** a different strategy..
17	adapt	(동) 맞추다, 조정하다, 적응하다 To remain competitive, the company has to be able to **adapt** to the changing marketplace.
18	calculate	(동) 계산하다 I'll just **calculate** the total.
19	produce	① (동) 생산하다 France **produces** a great deal of wine for export. ② (명) 농산물 The store sells fresh local **produce**.
	production	(명) 생산 We watched a video showing the various stages in the **production** of glass.
	productive	(형) 생산적인 We had a very **productive** meeting – I felt we solved lots of problems. cf) productivity: 생산성
20	appoint	(동) 지명하다 He's just been **appoint**ed as director of the publishing division.

🎙 기내방송　IN-FLIGHT SALES 1

　손님 여러분, 대한항공에서는 손님 여러분의 편리한 쇼핑을 위해, 우수한 품질의 다양한 면세품들을 일반 면세점보다 저렴한 환율로 판매하고 있습니다.

　구입을 원하시는 분은 카트가 지나갈 때에 말씀해 주시기 바랍니다.

　아울러, 면세품을 구매하실 때 중국 위안화를 사용하실 수 있으며, 위안화 현금수수 및 잔돈 지불은 10위안 이상 권 종으로만 사용 가능함을 알려드립니다.

　또한 국가명에서 환승하시는 손님 중에 액체류를 구입하기 원하시는 분은 승무원에게 문의하시거나, 기내지 SKY SHOP을 참고하시기 바랍니다.

Ladies and gentlemen,

Our in-flight duty free sales have started and you may now purchase duty free items or order items for your return flight.

Passengers transferring from 국가명 should contact with cabin crew when purchasing duty free liquor items.

For more information, please refer to the 'SKY SHOP' magazine in your seat pocket.

If you need any assistance, our cabin crew is happy to help you.

 기내방송　IN-FLIGHT SALES 2: 종료 안내

안내 말씀 드리겠습니다.

착륙에 필요한 안전업무 수행을 위해 면세품 판매를 마치겠습니다.

구입을 하지 못하신 분께서는 양해해 주시기 바랍니다. 감사합니다.

Ladies and gentlemen

We regret to announce that we have to close our duty free sales in preparation for landing.

Your understanding is appreciated.

Airline TOEIC Intro
Essential TOEIC &
Cabin Crew English

CHAPTER

06

능동태와 수동태

능동태와 수동태란?

영어는 강조하고 싶은 요소를 문장의 앞부분에 놓는다. 주어가 동사의 주체 혹은 행위자가 아니고 다른 대상에 의해 "···되어 지다"의 의미로 해석된다.

> 영림이가 연필을 **부러뜨렸다**. (능동태)   연필이 **부러졌다**. (수동태)

> : 문장 주어가 행위의 주체가 되는 것을 **능동태**라 하고, 주어가 다른 대상으로부터 행위를 당하는 것을 **수동태**라고 한다.

능동태 문장을 수동태 문장으로 바꾸는 방법

① 능동태 문장의 목적어가 수동태 문장의 주어로

② 능동태 문장의 동사는 be+과거분사 형태로

③ 능동태 문장의 주어는 문미에 by+목적격 형태로 바꾼다.

ex. He wrote the book. → The book was written by him.

---

1 수동태의 기본 형태: 'be 동사 + p.p.과거분사'

* 능동태의 시제와 동일한 시제를 유지한다.

* 진행시제: be + being + p.p.

* 완료시제: have has + been + P.P.

2 능동태와 수동태 구별 방법: 동사 뒤의 목적어 유무!

동사 뒤에 목적어가 있으면 능동태, 동사 뒤에 목적어가 없으면 수동태가 온다.

Tip 목적어를 취하지 않는 자동사는 수동태를 만들 수가 없다!

arrive, rise, remain, exist, disappear, happen, occur, take place, grow .....
ex. The prices **have been risen** 20% during the past year. → **have risen**

3 by가 아닌 다른 전치사와 함께 쓰는 수동태 관용적인 표현

(1) 전치사 in과 함께 쓰는 수동태 표현

> be engaged in~에 종사하다, 관여하다   be interested in~에 관심이 있다
> be involved in~에 관련되다

(2) 전치사 to와 함께 쓰는 수동태 표현

> be dedicated to ~에 헌신하다   be exposed to ~에 노출되다   be related to ~와 관계가 있다

(3) 전치사 at과 함께 쓰는 수동태 표현

> be surprised at ~에 놀라다   be shocked at~에 충격을 받다   be frightened at ~에 놀라다

(4) 전치사 with와 함께 쓰는 수동태 표현

> be dissatisfied with~에불만족하다   be pleased with~에 기뻐하다
> be equipped with~을 갖추고 있다

Tip

1. 4형식 동사의 수동태는 2개의 수동태 문장으로 만들 수 있다!

① 간접 목적어를 수동태의 주어로

ex. My father gave me the book. → I **was given the book** by my father.
(수동태 동사형태 위에도 명사 그대로 옴)

② 직접 목적어를 수동태의 주어로

ex. My father gave me the book. → The book **was given to me** by my father.
(간접 목적어 앞에 전치사 필요)

☞ 일반적으로 be 동사 뒤에 ~ing 형태는 능동태라서 뒤에 목적어(명사)가 있어야 된다고 생각하고 be동사 뒤에 과거분사가 오면 수동태형태라서 뒤에 목적어가 보이면 안 된다고 판단하고 문제를 풀지만, 4형식 문장은 be+p.p 뒤에 명사가 보이기도 하므로 주의해야한다!

2. 5형식 동사의 수동태

ex. The students called their teacher Tom. → Their teacher **was called Tom** by the students. (목적보어가 명사일 때 주의)

3. that 절을 목적어로 하는 동사의 수동태

주어+be expected / reminded / said / believed / advised / informed ..... + that

ex. It **is thought that** the company is planning a new ad campaign.
☞ be+p.p 뒤에 목적절 that이하가 온 게 아님. It은 가주어 that절은 진짜주어.
ex. He was informed that the meeting had been delayed.
☞ be+p.p 뒤에 목적절 that이하가 온 게 아님. that절은 4형식 문장의 직접목적어.

Grammar Practice

01 Denver Dam was _____ with steel beams over the spring to prevent annual summer overflow last year.

(A) reinforce

(B) reinforced

(C) reinforcing

(D) to reinforce

02 All the students who are _____ about the future career path will be invited to a job conference next month.

(A) concerns

(B) concerned

(C) concerning

(D) concerning

03 Our new film magazine _____ on March 1 focusing on Asian rising directors.

(A) will be published

(B) publishes

(C) will publish

(D) published

04 Once the plant in South Carolina has been _____, the management of Utizon Corporation expects its productivity to increase significantly,

(A) renovation

(B) renovating

(C) renovate

(D) renovated

05 As Joe is _____ to brief the new project to the board he may need to attend the meeting.

(A) expected

(B) expectation

(C) expecting

(D) expectant

06 During business hours, the use of company computers for personal use is strictly prohibited _____ management.

(A) on

(B) by

(C) until

(D) of

07 A portion of Sunflower Food's entire budget for 2021 _____ for the support of employees' health care.

(A) reserving

(B) has been reserved

(C) has reserved

(D) reserved

08 Orientation magazine _____ invaluable advice and information about traveling in Asia for over the decade.

(A) have been provided

(B) will be provided

(C) to provide

(D) has been providing

09 Free unlimited access to our Web site and online article archive _____ with subscription.

(A) includes

(B) including

(C) is included

(D) are included

10 Those who are looking for jobs are _____ to bring at least 10 resumes to the job fair and to be ready for short interviews.

(A) advised

(B) criticized

(C) monitored

(D) excused

Grammar Review TEST

01 At tomorrow's Mr. Lee retirement party, he _____ for his 40 years of hard work and dedication to the company.

(A) honore

(B) will be honored

(C) to be honored

(D) was honored

02 Our Company reported that its annual operating expenses _____ steady compared to those of last year.

(A) is remaining

(B) have remained

(C) to remain

(D) were remained

03 Jason and his staff collaborated to ensure that the 10th anniversary ceremony of H&M Group was well _____ .

(A) organizing

(B) organized

(C) organization

(D) organize

04 Ms. Miller was highly _____ for the customer service manager by the renowned HR team.

(A) recommendation

(B) recommended

(C) recommend

(D) recommending

05 Once next year's budget proposal _____ , the final decisions will be made by department managers.

(A) has been approved

(B) approves

(C) will approve

(D) approved

06 As the City Hall's parking lot _____ , visitors are strongly encouraged to use public transportation.

(A) repairs

(B) in repairing

(C) has repaired

(D) is being repaired

07 Customers are advised _____ this medicine in a cool, dry place after unsealing the bottle.

(A) store

(B) stores

(C) storing

(D) to store

08 Everyone attending the symposium on the Effects of Global Warming _____ a letter regarding the schedule.

(A) was sending

(B) would send

(C) sent

(D) was sent

09 Linda was very _____ with my brother's report on the latest fashion trends, so she hired him as a full time worker.

(A) pleased

(B) pleasant

(C) pleasing

(D) pleasure

10 At Effective Marketing Strategies workshop, Dr. Lee will _____ ways to achieve special marketing objectives.

(A) addressed

(B) be addressed

(C) address

(D) addressing

TOEIC ESSENTIAL VOCA

	필수어휘	의미 및 예문
1	budget	(명) 예산 The school **budget** is going to be cut again this year. (형) 매우 싼 **budget** airlines (=Low Cost carriers)
2	enclose	(동) 둘러싸다, 동봉하다. The park that **encloses** the monument has recently been enlarged. Please **enclose** a resume with your application.
3	in person	(부) 직접, 몸소 He delivered it **in person**.
4	refer reference	(동) 참고하다, 언급하다 (to) Don't **refer** to the matter again. (명) 참조, 언급, 조회, 추천서 My ex-boss wrote me a good **reference**.
5	publicize	(동) 알리다, 홍보하다 Luna has helped **publicize** the problem of homelessness.
6	periodical	(명) 정기간행물 She wrote several legal **periodicals**.
7	tax incentive	(명) 세제 혜택 **Tax incentives** worth millions brought dozens of companies and thousands of new jobs to the region last year.
8.	on a first-come, first-served basis	(부) 선착순으로 Meals are served **on a first-come, first-served basis**.
9	state-of-the-art	(형) 최첨단의 (=**cutting-edge**) The control panel is considered **state-of-the-art**.
10	reside residence resident	(동) 거주하다 The family **reside**s in Arkansas. (명) 주택, 거주지, 체류 10 Downing Street is the British Prime Minister's official **residence**. (명) 거주자 The local **resident**s were angry at the lack of parking spaces.

	필수어휘	의미 및 예문
11	financial	(형) 재정적인 (=fiscal) She organizes her **financial** affairs very efficiently.
12	retail	(명) 소매 The clothing company has six **retail** outlets in Perth..
13	wholesale	(명) 도매 (형,부) 도매로 We only sell **wholesale**, not to the public.
14	surpass	(동) sur+pass (넘어+지나다)→능가하다, 넘어서다 The book's success has **surpass**ed everyone's expectations.
15	approve approval	(동) 찬성하다, 승인하다 Do you **approve** of my idea? (명) 찬성, 승인 He showed his **approval** by smiling broadly.
16	supervise	(동) super+vise (위에서+보다) → 지도, 감독하다(=**oversee**) My job is to **supervise** the packing of all mail orders.
17	policy	(명) 정책. The oil markets are affected by economic **policy**.
18	experienced	(형) 경험있는 → 숙련된 (=**skilled**) A number of **experienced** candidates applied for this job position.
19	authority	(명) 권한, 당국 (복수로) The UN has used its **authority** to restore peace in the area. The health **authorities** are investigating the problem..
20	association	(명) 협회 The British Medical **Association** is campaigning for a complete ban on tobacco advertising.

손님 여러분,

A. 비행기가 흔들리고 있습니다.

B. 기류가 불안정합니다.

좌석벨트를 매주시기 바랍니다.

감사합니다.

Ladies and gentlemen,

We are experiencing turbulence.

Please return to your seat and fasten your seatbelt.

[좌석벨트 표시등이 켜진 채, 장시간 흔들린 경우]

손님 여러분, 비행기가 계속해서 흔들리고 있습니다.

좌석벨트를 매셨는지 다시 한번 확인해 주시고 화장실 사용은 삼가시기 바랍니다,

감사합니다.

Ladies and gentlemen,

We are continuing to experience turbulence.

For your safety, please remain seated with your seatbelt fastened.

Thank you.

[좌석벨트 표시등이 켜져 있으나 흔들리지 않는 경우 – 기장과 연락 후]

안내 말씀 드리겠습니다.

우리비행기는 잠시 후에 기류변화가 심한 지역을 지나갈 예정입니다. 좌석벨트를 계속 매주시

기 바랍니다.

Ladies and gentlemen,

The captain would like to inform you that we may still encounter some turbulence. please

remain seated with your seatbelt fastened until the seatbelt sigh has been turned off.

Thank you

Airline TOEIC Intro
Essential TOEIC &
Cabin Crew English

CHAPTER
07

시제

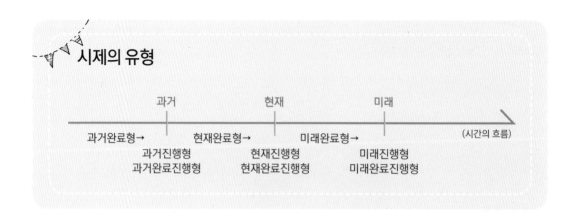

시제의 유형

과거 · 현재 · 미래 (시간의 흐름)

과거완료형→ · 현재완료형→ · 미래완료형→
과거진행형 · 현재진행형 · 미래진행형
과거완료진행형 · 현재완료진행형 · 미래완료진행형

---

1 단순시제

특정한 시간에 발생한 일이나 상태를 나타내는 시제

	현재 (Present)	과거 (Past)	미래 (Future)
단순 (Simple)	단순현재	단순과거	단순미래
진행 (Progressive)	현재진행	과거진행	미래진행
완료 (Perfect)	현재완료	과거완료	미래완료

2 진행시제

주어진 시점에서 움직임이 계속 진행 중임을 나타내는 시제

현재진행	am/is/are+ing	He is reading a book.	현재 동작이나 상태의 계속, 가까운 미래	now, right now
과거진행	was/were+ing	He was reading a book.	과거 특정 시점에 진행되고 있었던 일	과거시점 나타내는 시간표현
미래진행	will be+ing	He will be reading a book.	미래 특정 시점에 진행되고 있을 사건, 동작	미래시점 나타내는 시간표현

3 완료시제

기준 시점보다 앞선 시점부터 발생한 일이나 상태가 기준 시점까지 계속되는 것을 나타내는 시제

현재완료	have/has+p.p	I have lived here for 2 years.	과거에 발생한 일이 현재까지 상태나 동작이 이어지는 경우	since+연도 / over the last, past+ 기간 / for+기간
과거완료	had+p.p	I had lived here for 2 years.	과거보다 앞서 발생한 사건은 과거완료로 표기	과거 특정시점 나타내는 표현
미래완료	will have+p.p	I will have lived here for 2 years by next year.	미래의 어느 특정 시점을 기준으로 하여 그때까지 완료됨을 나타냄	by next + 시간표현 / by the end of + 시간표현 / next+시간표현

Tip

1. 시간, 조건 부사절에서는 현재가 미래를 대신함

   ex. The show will begin as soon as the magician **arrives**.
   ex. If it **rains** tomorrow, we will stay at home.

2. by + 명사 / by the time S + V (미래시점) 나오면 답은 미래 완료가 됨

3. 요구, 주장, 명령의 동사와 이성적 판단의 형용사, 명사 + that 절에서 동사는 동사원형!

   – that 절 뒤 주어 + 동사 사이에 should 가 생략되어 있기 때문임
   ask, require, demand, insist, recommend, important, essential, necessary, imperative
   ex. He **requested that** any changes of the contract be sent to his secretary by tonight.
   ex. It is **important** that she drink a lot of water everyday for her recovery. (drinks)

4. 가정법에서는 시제 일치의 원칙이 적용이 안 됨

   ex. If I **were** you, I **would accept** the job.
   ex. If I **had had** more time, I **would have done** it better.

01 Mr. Wanga _____ to study business at NYU four years ago while working at Boston Company.

(A) started

(B) is starting

(C) starts

(D) has started

02 Accidents at the Hillside Apartment construction site have been continuously reduced since the new safety regulation procedures _____ implemented.

(A) were

(B) to be

(C) will be

(D) been

03 Finn Air _____ a press conference once the management has decided whether or not to merge with Hong Kong Air.

(A) is held

(B) hold

(C) will hold

(D) has been held

04 Before the Marketing Department started a promotion campaign, some interns _____ to help the employees to survey the market.

(A) recruits

(B) were recruited

(C) will recruit

(D) had recruited been

05 My lawyer _____ the file if you need to modify it for approval.

(A) is reviewing

(B) review

(C) reviewing

(D) will review

06 Orange Design Firm _____ to develop the urban outdated parking lots for a long time.

(A) work

(B) have worked

(C) has been working

(D) is working

07 Whatever your company's need may be, you _____ the best strategies from MC Business Solutions.

(A) receive

(B) has received

(C) will receive

(D) received

08 Luky Star Corporation _____ expanding its size before it was named one of the best small businesses in the sports goods industry.

(A) has not considered

(B) were not considered

(C) will not consider

(D) had not considered

09 All applicants are asked to show which licenses they _____ and what language they speak before the interview.

(A) had possessed

(B) possess

(C) possessing

(D) will possess

10 Sales of Max & Co. Inc. _____ in the last two years mainly due to its incresingly popular new line of clothing.

(A) double

(B) has doubled

(C) have doubled

(D) to double

01 To simplify the complicated process of filling travel expense reports, the accounting manager _____ implementing the new procedures last month.

(A) suggesting

(B) suggested

(C) suggests

(D) suggest

02 Our IT technicians _____ the company's computers and networking system every month to prevent viruses.

(A) checks

(B) checked

(C) check

(D) to check

03 The international market for organic products _____ to more than twice its current size in the next decade.

(A) grew

(B) growing

(C) has grown

(D) will grow

04 Greenland Golf Club _____ among the best golf clubs in Australia over the last five years.

(A) has ranked

(B) is ranking

(C) ranked

(D) would rank

05. Once all of the entries have been received by the end of this week, we _____ the winning slogan.

(A) will choose

(B) was choosing

(C) chose

(D) has chosen

06 Box Corporation's sales of music playing software have increased by 20 percent _____ the last six months.

(A) in (B) on

(C) at (D) of

07 As the manager is ready to place another order, Startrack Office Supplies _____ a new price list.

(A) published (B) publishing

(C) had published (D) will have published

08 My assistant _____ the budget proposal if you need to send it for approval by Tuesday.

(A) is reviewing (B) will review

(C) reviews (D) reviewed

09 Last year, Netflex's Quality Control Department _____ several new policies to improve production efficiency.

(A) implementation (B) implements

(C) implemented (D) implementing

10 Whatever your company's needs may be, you _____ the best care and attention to detail from Han Business Solutions.

(A) is received (B) has received

(C) will receive (D) would have received

	필수어휘	의미 및 예문
1	oversee	(동) over+see (위에서+보다) → 감독하다 (supervise) He was appointed to **oversee** the project.
2	revenue	(명) 총수입 It is expected that first-quarter **revenue** will be $50 million.
3	withdraw	(동) with+draw (멀리(=away)+당기다) → (뒤로) 물러나다, 철수하다, (돈) 인출하다, 취소하다 Do not **withdraw** your money from your account.
4	remarkably	(부) 주목할만하게, 눈에 띄게 You have performed **remarkably**.
5	economical	(형) 경제적인, 실속 있는 What is the most **economical** way of heating this house?
6	economic	(형) 경제의, 경제에 관련된 The government's **economic** policies have led us into the worst recession in years.
7	arrange	(동) 정리/정렬하다, 준비하다 The meeting has been **arrange**d for Wednesday.
8	commuter	(명) 통근자, 통학자 The train was packed with commuters.
9	claim	① (동) 요구하다, (사실로) 주장하다 The company **claim**s that it is not responsible for the pollution in the river. ② (명) 주장, 요구, 권리 The government's **claim** that it would reduce taxes proved false.
10	demand	① (동) 요구하다 I **demand**ed an explanation. ② (명) 요구, 수요
11	meet	(동) (요구, 필요, 기한) 충족시키다 We haven't yet been able to find a house that **meets our needs/ requirements**. Do you think we will be able to **meet our deadline/target**?

필수어휘	의미 및 예문
12 expense expenses	(명) 비용, 지출 (단수) We went on holiday at my **expense**. (명) (특정한 목적에 사용되는) 경비 (복수) living **expenses**; medical **expenses**; legal **expenses**, etc.
13 colleague	(명) 동료 (=coworker) Please read this memo carefully and hand it on to your **colleague**s.
14 statistics	(명) 통계 **Statistics** show that women live longer than men.
15 procedure	(명) 절차, 순서 You must follow correct **procedure** at all times. cf) 어떤 일을 수행하기위해 따르게 되는 보편적인 수순. 예를 들어, 장학금을 받기 　위해서는 통상적으로 따라야 할 것들이 있다. 성적을 잘 받고, 신청서를 작성하고, 　심사를 받고 등등. 장학금을 받기 위해 해야 할 이런 절차를 procedure라고 한다. (A procedure is about how we do something.)
16 process	(명) 과정 It's all part of the learning **process**. cf) 어떤 결과물을 얻기 위한 일련의 과정. 예를 들어, 하나의 자동차를 만들어내기 위해서는 처음부터 끝까지 정해진 일련의 순서가 있는데 이것을 process라고 이해하면 된다. (A process is about what we do.)
17 be committed to	(동) 헌신하다. He was committed to world peace. cf) A is committed to B 　　　　devoted 　　　　dedicated
18 undergo	(동) under+go (밑을+가다) (힘든일을) 겪다 I **underwent** an operation on a tumor in my brain.
19 merger	(명) 합병 The **merger** of these two companies would create the world's biggest accounting firm. cf) M&A: Merger and Acquisition
20 resume résumé	(동) [rɪˈzuːm] (멈춘 것을) 재개하다 Normal services will be **resume**d in the spring. (명) [ˈrezəmeɪ] 이력서 (=CV) She sent her **resume** to 50 companies, but didn't even get an interview.

안내 말씀 드리겠습니다.

대한민국에 입국하시는 손님 여러분께서는 입국에 필요한 휴대품 신고서를 다시 한번 확인 해 주십시오. 그리고 미화 만불 이상, 또는 이에 해당하는 외화를 갖고 계시거나/ 미화 400불 이상의 물품을 구입하신 분은 그 내용을 휴대품 신고서에 반드시 신고해 주시기 바랍니다. 또한 국내 구제역 확산 방지를 위해 해외에서 가축농장을 방문하셨거나 축산물을 가져오신 분은 가까운 검역기관에 신고해 주시기 바랍니다. 또한 지금부터 헤드폰과 잡지는 걷으오니 협조해 주시기 바랍니다.

Ladies and gentlemen,

All passengers entering Korea are requested to have your entry documents ready. If you are carrying foreign currency more than 10,00 US dollars, or if you acquired more than 400 US dollars worth of articles abroad, please declare them on the customs form.

🎙 기내방송 ARRIVAL INFORMATION: KOREA 2

안내 말씀 드리겠습니다.

대한민국에 입국하시는 손님 여러분께서는 입국에 필요한 휴대품 신고서를 작성하셨는지 확인하여 주시기 바랍니다. 그리고 미화 만 불 이상, 또는 이에 해당하는 외화를 갖고 계시거나 600불 이상의 구매한 물품을 지니고 계신 분은 휴대품 신고서에 반드시 신고해주시기 바랍니다. 육류, 과일 및 다른 음식 물품도 신고해야 합니다. 신고를 하지 않는 경우는 가산세가 부과될 수 있습니다.

Ladies and gentlemen,

All passengers entering Korea are requested to have your entry documents ready. If you carry foreign currency more than 10.000 US dollars, or if you purchased more than 600 dollars worth of articles abroad, please declare them on the customs form. Also, meats, plants, fruits or any other food items should be declared. Failure to declare could result in an additional tax.

형용사와 부사

형용사란?

예쁜 꽃
형용사
a beautiful flower

꽃이 예쁘다
형용사
The flower is beautiful.

1 형용사 형태

형용사는 주로 -able, -sive, -ous, -tic, -y와 같은 꼬리말로 끝난다.

2 형용사 기능

(1) 형용사의 한정용법: 명사 앞 또는 뒤에서 수식

(2) 형용사의 서술용법: 주격, 목적격 보어

(3) 수량 형용사

many, few, a few, a number of	+ 가산 복수 명사
much, little, a little, an amount of	+ 불가산 명사
each, every	+ 단수 명사
a lot of, plenty of	+ 가산/불가산 명사

3 혼동되는 형용사 어휘

beneficial	유익한	beneficent	인정 많은
considerable	상당한	considerate	사려 깊은
successful	성공의	successive	연속의

respective	각각의	respectful	공손한
comparable	필적하는	comparative	비교의
comprehensible	알기 쉬운	comprehensive	포괄적인
responsible	책임지는	responsive	반응하는
sensitive	민감한	sensible	분별 있는

4 토익 빈출 형용사

durable	내구성 있는	optimistic	낙관적인
satisfactory result	만족스러운 결과	attached	첨부된
competitive	경쟁력 있는	consecutive	연속의
a reasonable price	합리적인 가격	relevant	연관된
reliable information	믿을만한 정보	existing equipment	기존의 장비
potential customers	잠재적 고객들	missing luggage	잃어버린 짐
complicated procedures	복잡한 절차들	a demanding job	까다로운 일
in a timely manner	시기적절한	dedicated workers	헌신적인 근로자
understanding teacher	이해심 많은 교사	an opposing point of view	반대하는 관점
qualified members	자격있는 회원들	preferred means	선호되어지는 방법들
protective equipment	보호 장비	designated area	지정된 지역
accessible	접속 가능한	detailed information	세부적인 정보
critical	비판적인,중요한	rewarding job	보람을 주는 일
numerable	수많은	an enclosed letter	동봉된 편지

✓ Check Up Test

1. Linda is an especially _____ employee at YM Inc.

   (A) value   (B) values   (C) valuably   (D) valuable

2. My staff and I would like to express _____ gratitude for all your hard work.

   (A) my   (B) your   (C) our   (D) their

부사란?

형용사, 동사, 다른 부사 또는 문장 전체를 수식하여 의미를 강조하거나 풍부하게 하는 것

lately(최근에), highly(매우), nearly(거의), closely(자세히), mostly(대개), hardly(거의~않다)

1 부사의 역할

동사 수식	He completed the project effectively.
형용사 수식	It is relatively difficult that this legislation will be passed.
부사 수식	He behaved extremely badly.
준동사 수식	The newly installed computer is out of order.
문장 전체 수식	Finally, he overcame lung cancer.

① 형용사 + ly
Ex. Completely, entirely, likely, approximately

② 형용사와 부사가 같은 형태
Ex. Fast 빠른 – 빠르게 early 이른 – 이르게
long 긴 – 오랫동안 far 먼 – 멀리
hard 딱딱한 – 열심히 enough 충분한 – 충분하게

③ 기타
Well 잘 too 너무 already 이미 just 단지

2 부사와 형용사의 형태가 같은 경우

hard / fast / high / late / near / early ....

ex. I was **late** for the class.(형용사) He prepared the meeting **late** at night.

3 접속 부사: 접속사처럼 문장의 의미를 연결해주는 기능은 하지만 부사이다.

consequently, furthermore, hence, however, moreover, nevertheless, otherwise, therefore

ex. She likes the car. **However,** she can't buy it.

She likes the car **but** she can't buy it.

4 부정부사: hardly / rarely / seldom

ex. I had **hardly** any time.

I could **seldom** understand him.

☞ 부정부사가 문두에 나오면 도치 (부정부사+V+S)

ex. **Hardly** has the situation been more urgent than now.

✓ Check Up Test

1. Customer feedback is becoming an _____ essential factor in planning a new project.

(A) increase   (B) increases   (C) increasing   (D) increasingly

2. All managers in the company agreed that Tom works _____.

(A) conscientiously   (B) conscientious

(C) conscientiousness   (D) conscience

다음 각 부사의 뜻을 아래에서 찾아보시오.

1. Completely	(	)	2. Adequately	(	)
3. Activery	(	)	4. Frequently	(	)
5. Temporarily	(	)	6. Significantly	(	)
7. Dramatically	(	)	8. Favorably	(	)
9. Sharply	(	)	10. Suddenly	(	)

급격하게 적극적으로 완전히 극적으로 빈번하게 현저하게 일시적으로 갑자기 적절하게 순조롭게

01 Employees on domestic assignment with Franklin foundation receive _____ support when finding a place to live.

(A) financial   (B) financially

(C) finance   (D) finances

02 All Pasadena residents are requested to clean the garbage cans _____ with hot water.

(A) periodic   (B) periodically

(C) periodical   (D) period

03 Morgan Motors _____ invests in research and development so its technology is behind its competitors by more than five years.

(A) rare   (B) rarer

(C) rarest   (D) rarely

04 This guide provides you with _____ information about your accommodations and tourist attractions .

(A) comprehensive   (B) comprehensible

(C) comprehending   (D) comprehend

05 Full-time workers who work flexible hours are more _____ than expected.

(A) producing   (B) produced

(C) productive   (D) productively

06 Kenzi began his career as a sales representative but now he is a _____ renowned businessperson in the world.

(A) nation

(B) nationality

(C) national

(D) nationally

07 It is _____ to buy tickets early because many of last year's performances were sold out before the event.

(A) advice

(B) advisory

(C) advisable

(D) advisably

08 Tahoma Inc. recently decided to switch its suppliers because TPC Inc. has been _____ late in shipping their orders.

(A) consistently

(B) sensibly

(C) steadily

(D) exactly

09 The senior manager revised the report submitted by Ms. Johansen because the language in it was too _____ .

(A) repeat

(B) repetitive

(C) repeating

(D) repetition

10 Enclosed you will find a new membership card and a copy of your contact information as it _____ appears in your membership record.

(A) lately

(B) availably

(C) significantly

(D) currently

01 A recent survey shows that Luna's new electronic models are more _____ than the previous ones.

(A) dependability

(B) depending

(C) depended

(D) dependable

02 Everyone would go into the auditorium for assembly and then go to their _____ classes.

(A) respective

(B) respectful

(C) respected

(D) respect

03 According to the report released today, retail sales in furnishing goods declined in March after a significant _____ in February.

(A) increase

(B) impression

(C) access

(D) accent

04 Jeffersen Motors' sales figures in the third quarter were nearly _____ to those recorded in the first quarter..

(A) uniform

(B) equal

(C) even

(D) fair

05 In any case, lawyers are typically _____ to take on such cases because they are time-consuming and difficult.

(A) reliant

(B) reluctant

(C) available

(D) predominant

06 Due to a concerned effort in recent years by the stores to attract _____ shoppers, this shopping mall is slowly changing.

(A) individually

(B) individuals

(C) individual

(D) individualize

07 Mr. Brown, the guest speaker, will deliver a speech on effective overseas marketing _____ after the keynote speech by the chairman.

(A) almost

(B) immediately

(C) sometimes

(D) infrequently

08 This is the third _____ weekly fall, following the encouraging cooperation between the divisions.

(A) successive

(B) immediately

(C) successful

(D) infrequent

09 The new CEO considered it _____ to stop all the manufacture lines while safety inspections were being conducted.

(A) necessity

(B) necessary

(C) necessarily

(D) necessitate

10 The display panel is designed to ensure that the warning lights are _____ visible from a distance.

(A) clear

(B) clearness

(C) clearly

(D) clean

계속해서 이 비행기로 도시 이름 까지 가시는 손님 분들께 안내방송 드립니다. _____ 공항에 도착하시면 모든 짐을 갖고 내리시고 탑승권도 잊지 마시기 바랍니다. 내리신 후에는 잠시 공항 대기실에서 기다려 주시기 바랍니다. 이 비행기는 _____ 시 _____ 분에 다시 출발하며, 탑승시각은 다시 알려드리겠습니다.

Ladies and gentlemen,

Passengers continuing to 도시 이름 with us should take all your belongings with you including your boarding pass when you leave the aircraft.

After leaving the airplane, proceed to the transit area.

Our scheduled departure time for 도시 이름 is _____ : _____.

We will start re-boarding in abut _____ minutes and announce the boarding time.

안내 말씀 드리겠습니다.

인천공항에 도착 후 여러분께서 내리실 Gate는 10번입니다.

계속해서 연결편으로 여행하시는 손님 여러분께 출발 탑승구를 안내해 드리겠습니다.

도쿄행 대한항공 701편은 12번 탑승구

파리행 901편 24번, 런던행 대한항공 907편은 30번 탑승구에서 출발할 예정입니다.

문의사항이 있는 분께서는 저희 승무원에게 말씀해 주십시오.

Ladies and gentlemen,

We will be arriving at gate number in Incheon international airport.

Also, we will now provide connecting gate information.

Korean Air flight 701 to ToKyo, gate 12, KE 901 to Paris, gate 24,

KE 907 to London, gate 30.

For further information, please contact one of one of our crew.

비교급과 최상급

비교에는 원급, 비교급, 최상급이 있다.

원급 구문	as 원급 as	as large as
비교급 구문	비교급 + than	larger than
최상급 구문	the + 최상급 (단, 부사의 최상급 앞에는 the를 쓰지 않음)	the largest

ex. The impact has been felt hardest by small-to mid-sized employers. – 부사의 최상급

1 비교급과 최상급은 형용사와 부사의 급에 따라 형태를 변화시켜 만든다.

- 2음절 이하는 -er, -est, 3음절은 more, most가 붙는 규칙 변화를 한다.

형용사 / 부사 (원급)	비교급	최상급
fast	faster	fastest
diligent	more diligent	most diligent
good/well	better	best
bad	worse	worst
many/much	more	most
little	less	least

2 비교 관용 표현

as soon as possible	가능한 한 빨리
not so much A as B	A라기보다는 오히려 B
as much as	①~정도,~만큼 ②사실상~, 거의~
no more	더 이상 ~하지 않다
no more A than B	B처럼 A하지 않다
no more than	겨우(=only)
the + 비교급~, the + 비교급~	~하면 할수록 더 ~하다
the + 비교급 + of the two	둘 중 더~한
at one's best	가장 좋은 상태에
one of the 최상급 +복수명사	가장 ~한 사람/것 중 하나
the+서수+최상급	몇 번째로 가장 ~한

ex. Busan is **the second <u>largest</u>** city in Korea.

ex. Most resumes are read for **no more than** a few seconds.
(대부분의 이력서들은 겨우 몇 초 동안만 읽혀진다.)

3 비교를 강조, 수식해주는 부사

원급	very, nearly, almost, just
비교급	much, even, still, far, a lot, a little, a bit, by far, slightly
최상급	much, far, the very, by far

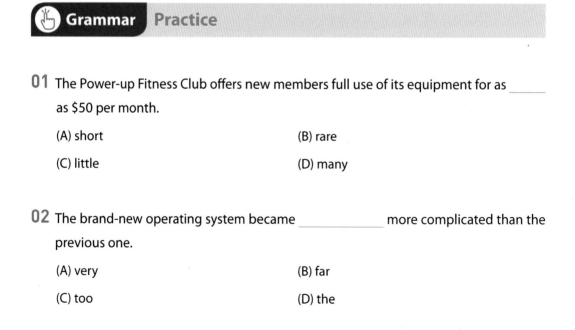

Check Up Test

1. The merger of Boston and New York Solutions created one of _____ extensive financial services companies in the world.

    (A) most   (B) the most   (C) best   (D) the best

    ☞ in the world의 어구를 유의하여 최상급인지 판단하자.

2. Many analysts reported that the Internet is not so much a new technology _____ a new medium.

    (A) as   (B) so   (C) than   (D) more

3. Many companies are burdened by high taxes and requirements that are more _____ than those of other states.

    (A) restrictive   (B) restrict   (C) restrictively   (D) to restrict

Grammar Practice

01 The Power-up Fitness Club offers new members full use of its equipment for as _____ as $50 per month.

   (A) short   (B) rare

   (C) little   (D) many

02 The brand-new operating system became _____ more complicated than the previous one.

   (A) very   (B) far

   (C) too   (D) the

03 The TV commercial of DUC motors is more _____ than the one of its competitor company.

(A) memorable

(B) memorize

(C) memorably

(D) memory

04 Kaplan Inc. is the _____ microwave oven manufacturer in the world.

(A) large

(B) largely

(C) largest

(D) most large

05 Most customers prefer to be contacted by email _____ in person.

(A) later than

(B) rather than

(C) no sooner than

(D) no longer

06 After the disk driver is installed, the protective cover should be removed as _____ as possible to prevent the accumulation of dust.

(A) quick

(B) quicker

(C) quickly

(D) quickest

07 The new word processing program will help not only office workers but also students work more _____ .

(A) efficiently

(B) efficient

(C) efficiency

(D) efficiencies

08 Customers are advised to be as specific _____ possible when they have problems with the product they purchased.

(A) more

(B) even

(C) than

(D) as

09 The 123-story building is one of the _____ popular tourist attractions in the city.

(A) much   (B) most   (C) ever   (D) best

10 The current transportation system is superior _____ the previous one.

(A) to   (B) than   (C) as   (D) for

💡 Grammar Review TEST

01 Any changes to your reservation should be made three days _____ your arrival.

(A) prior to   (B) after

(C) than   (D) as

02 TasteGood Bakery announced its fourth quarter's earnings were _____ than those for the third quarter.

(A) high   (B) highest

(C) highly   (D) higher

03 Sales of compact cars dropped by 25 percent in November, reflecting a somewhat _____ demand than expected..

(A) weakly   (B) weaken

(C) weaker   (D) weak

04 Mr. Baek is considered to have a fair chance to be promoted because he has worked the _____ of all the employees at Testa Lab.

(A) hardly   (B) hard

(C) hardest   (D) harder

05 I think the diamond at Toronto Auction might be the largest and the most expensive _____ found.

(A) that   (B) since

(C) than   (D) yet

06 PEAR Electronics will roll out its latest cell phone with cutting-edge functions next month and its price is expected to be _____ $2,500.

(A) as many as   (B) as much as

(C) as far as   (D) later than

07 Your application form must be postmarked _____ Friday, November 17th.

(A) in advance   (B) beforehand

(C) no later than   (D) afterward

08 A lot of public schools are switching to recycled paper because it is less _____ than new paper.

(A) expensiveness   (B) expense

(C) expensively   (D) expensive

09 As mentioned on the phone, your order will be delivered as _____ as possible.

(A) promptly   (B) scarcely

(C) highly   (D) remarkably

10 To meet the deadline, accountants at Lolli Inc. must hand in all financial documents by tomorrow at the _____ .

(A) lowest   (B) largest

(C) latest   (D) fastest

계속해서 이 비행기로 호놀룰루까지 가시는 손님 여러분께 안내 말씀 드리겠습니다.

나리타 국제공항에 도착하면 모든 짐을 갖고 내리시고 탑승권도 잊지 마시기 바랍니다.

내리신 후에는 공항 대기 장소에서 잠시 기다려 주십시오.

이 비행기의 다음 출발 시각은 9시 20분이며, 탑승시각은 공항에서 알려드리겠습니다.

감사합니다.

Ladies and gentlemen,

Passengers continuing on Honolulu with us should take all your belongings with you including boarding pass when you leave the airplane.

After leaving the aircraft,

proceed to the transit area.

Our scheduled departure time for is 9:20 _{am/pm}

We will start re-boarding in about minutes.

please listen for a boarding announcement in the transit area.

Thank you.

부정사

to 부정사란?

☞ 동사 '먹다'가 '먹는 것', '먹을', '먹기 위해' 등으로 바뀌어 문장에서 명사, 형용사, 부사 역할을 하는 것처럼, to + 동사원형의 형태로 문장 내에서 여러 역할을 하는 준동사의 일종

1 준동사의 개념

* 동사의 성질을 가지면서 문장에서 다른 품사 역할을 하는 것

- 동사에 따라 뒤에 목적어, 보어 취할 수 있음
- 시제, 태를 표현할 수 있음
- 행위 주체를 표현할 수 있음(의미상의 주어)
- 부사의 수식을 받을 수 있음

	부정사	동명사
형태	to + 동사원형	동사 + ing
기능	명사, 형용사, 부사	명사

2 부정사의 용법

명사적 용법 (~하기,~하는 것)	To see a movie is my hobby.	주어 자리
	I want to see a movie.	목적어 자리
	My hobby is to see a movie.	보어 자리
형용사적 용법 (~해야 할,~할)	He has a lot of things to do.	명사 수식
	I am to see a movie.	보어 자리
부사적 용법 (~하기 위해서)	He went abroad to study English.	동사 수식
	I am sorry to hear that.	형용사 수식
	To swim in the river, I practiced hard last summer.	문장 수식

3 부정사의 의미상의 주어

부정사의 행위 주체를 표현 할 필요가 있을 때 부정사 앞에 for + 목적격으로 표현한다.

cf) **사람의 성질**을 나타내는 **형용사 (nice, kind, smart, good ....)** 뒤는 <u>of + 목적격</u>

ex. It's time **for you** to go to work.

'그 문제는 우리가 풀기 어렵다'☞ 주어는 '그 문제'이지만 '푸는'사람은 '우리'이다. 이처럼 주어는 아니

지만 to 부정사를 행하는 주체를 to 부정사의 '의미상의 주어'라고 한다.

The problem is difficult for us to solve.

Tip 의미상의 주어를 표현하지 않는 경우!

① 의미상의 주어가 일반인일 경우
② 의미상의 주어와 문장의 주어가 동일한 경우
③ 의미상의 주어와 문장의 목적어가 동일한 경우

4 동사 + to부정사 부정사만을 목적어로 취하는 동사들

hope, wish, want, plan, expect, afford, offer, need, ask, agree, learn, choose, promise, decide, desire, fail, refuse

> ex. The supplier **offered to send** samples.
> ex. Some people **refuse to pay** their income taxes.

5 동사 + 목적어 + to부정사

ask, invite, remind, encourage, permit, allow, want, force, persuade, warn

> ex. The manager **encouraged us to think** creatively.

enable A to do	A가 ~할 수 있게 하다	invite A to do	A에게 ~하라고 초대하다
encourage A to do	A에게 ~하라고 권장하다/격려하다	require A to do	A에게 ~하라고 요구하다
persuade A to do	A에게 ~하라고 설득하다	request A to do	A에게 ~하라고 요청하다
instruct A to do	A에게 ~하라고 지시하다	remind A to do	A에게 ~하라고 상기시키다
ask A to do	A에게 ~해달라고 요청하다	warn A to do	A에게 ~하라고 경고하다/주의 주다
allow A to do	A에게 ~할 수 있게 허락하다	cause A to do	A에게 ~하도록 야기하다
advise A to do	A에게 ~하라고 조언하다	force A to do	A에게 ~하도록 강요하다

6 원형부정사

지각동사see, listen, fell, smell, ... & 사역동사have, make, let, help가 쓰인 5형식 문장에서 부정사가 목적보어 자리에 들어갈 때 to가 없는 동사원형원형부정사만 쓴다.

> 사역동사(make, let, have) + 목적어 + 원형부정사/과거분사
> help + 목적어 + 원형부정사/to부정사

지각동사(hear, watch, see) + 목적어 + 원형부정사/현재분사/과거분사

ex. I saw you dance. (or dancing) ☞ 둘 다 답으로 가능

ex. I had him go home. ☞ going or to go 는 오답

7 부정사 대신 쓰이는 가주어와 가목적어 it

부정사가 주어나 목적어 자리에 쓰일 때 가짜 주어_{목적어} it을 쓰고 부정사는 뒤로 보낸다.

ex. **To study English** is difficult. ☞ **It** is difficult **to study English**.

ex. I found **to study English** difficult. ☞ I found **it** difficult **to study English**.

8 관용적인 표현들

be able to	be ready to	
be about to	be scheduled to	
be eligible to	in an effort to	+ 동사원형
in order to	= so as to	
be likely to	be eager to	
be liable to	be reluctant to	

원형부정사가 쓰이는 관용구	
had better	
would rather	+ 동사원형
cannot but	

to 부정사의 수식을 받는 명사들		
ability to	means to	
chance to	opportunity to	+ 동사원형
effort to	right to	

✓ Check Up Test

1. Please fill out the evaluation form to let us _____ if our service system should be modified.

   (A) know   (B) knows   (C) to know   (D) knowing

2. It was not easy _____ the team to finish its work because so many employees were absent.

   (A) of   (B) to   (C) for   (D) with

☞ Grammar Practice

01 DUC Hotel has been committed to _____ excellent service to customers.

(A) give   (B) giving   (C) be given   (D) being given

02 It is very important _____ visitors to wear personal protective clothing including a safety helmet before entering the construction site.

(A) to   (B) many   (C) for   (D) the

03 Mr. Brown called this afternoon _____ Ms. Sylvia of the latest changes to the sick leave policy of the company.

(A) to announce   (B) informed   (C) notifying   (D) to inform

04 Dr. Stevenson would like _____ almost all of his students to the party that will be held in 107 Building tomorrow.

(A) to invite   (B) inviting   (C) invitingly   (D) invited

05 All candidates must be prepared _____ and have superior communication skills.

(A) relocate

(B) relocation

(C) to relocate

(D) relocating

06 He is looking for a job which will enables him _____ his skills.

(A) develop

(B) developed

(C) developed

(D) to develop

07 The purpose of this program is _____ participants with better understanding of the biological function of MSCs.

(A) provided

(B) provide

(C) providence

(D) to provide

08 Yellow Carpet helps pedestrians _____ roads safely.

(A) cross

(B) crossing

(C) crossed

(D) to be crossed

09 He makes _____ a rule to work out for 30 minutes after a meal almost every day.

(A) for

(B) out

(C) it

(D) up

10 The editor insisted that publication be suspended _____ some typographic errors in the article.

(A) correcting

(B) corrective

(C) correctively

(D) to correct

01 In an effort _____ security, the management is planning to install infrared sensors at the main entrance.

(A) improving

(B) improve

(C) improved

(D) to improve

02 The upgraded RAM will allow computer users _____ a lot of information at a time.

(A) will process

(B) to process

(C) processed

(D) processing

03 To handle the recent increase in sales, the CEO has decided _____ a number of new employees.

(A) recruit

(B) recruiting

(C) to be recruited

(D) to recruit

04 _____ the contents of our new magazine will undoubtedly help attract new readers.

(A) Diversity

(B) Diversification

(C) Diversifying

(D) Diversified

05 The new CFO did not let the current financial problems in the domestic market _____ the company's long-term plans.

(A) affect

(B) to affect

(C) affected

(D) to be affected

06 When applying for a house improvement loan, please remember _____ your house contract and a written renovation estimate together.

(A) submitting

(B) submit

(C) to submit

(D) submission

07 He left his house early in the morning in order _____ the heavy traffic.

(A) avoiding

(B) of avoidance

(C) to avoid

(D) to be avoided

08 Due to the recent increase in raw material prices, these companies have no choice but _____ higher fees to the customers.

(A) charge

(B) charged

(C) charging

(D) to charge

09 Those with good communications skills _____ to have good relationships with coworkers.

(A) attract

(B) seem

(C) force

(D) rely

10 Staff members at Stella restaurant are _____ to satisfying the needs of customers.

(A) expressed

(B) scheduled

(C) committed

(D) designed

필수어휘	의미 및 예문
1 **attach** (ad-: 부가)	(동) 붙이다, 첨부하다 (to) I **attached** a photo to my application form. cf) attachment: 첨부
2 **detach** (de-: 분리, 제거)	(동) 떼어 내다, 분리하다. You can **detach** the hood if you prefer the coat without it. cf) detachment: 제거, 분리
3 **distribution**	(명) 분배, 배분 There is an uneven **distribution** of wealth across the country..
4 **confirm**	(동) 확인하다 Flights should be **confirm**ed 48 hours before departure.
5 **supplies**	(명) 물품 We order office **supplies** every 2 weeks.

6 **encourage**	(동) en+courage (하게 하다+용기) → 용기를 갖게 하다, 독려하다
	We **encourage** the victims to talk freely about their experiences.
	cf) 접두사 혹은 접미사로 'en'을 붙이면 모두 동사를 만들어 "~하게 만들다"라는
	의미를 갖게 한다.
	e.g. weak+en: 약화시키다
	      sad+(D)en: 슬프게 만들다
	      en+able: 가능하게 하다
	      en+sure: 확실하게하다
	      en+danger: 위험에 빠뜨리다
	      en+large: 확대시키다
	      en+rich: 풍요롭게하다
	      em+power: 권한을 갖게 하다

7 **socialize**	(동) 사귀다, 어울리다 I don't tend to **socialize** with my colleagues much
8. **administrative**	(형) 관리상의, 행정상의 **Administrative** work involves organizing and supervising an organization or institution.
9 **in advance**	(부) 미리, 사전에 If you're going to come, please let me know **in advance**.
10 **assume**	① (동) 추정하다 (=suppose) Don't always **assume** the worst. ② (동) (책임) 떠맡다 (=take over) The new president **assume**s office at midnight tonight.

	필수어휘	의미 및 예문
11	turnover	① (명) 총매상 (=revenue) Large supermarkets have high **turnover**s. ② (명) 이직률 The large number of temporary contracts resulted in a high **turnover** of staff.
12	thorough	(형) 꼼꼼한, 세심한 (=meticulous) They did a **thorough** search of the area but found nothing. cf) thoroughly: 꼼꼼하게 (=meticulously)
13	aware	(형) 알고 있는 (of; that ~) Were you **aware** of the speed you were driving at? I wasn't even **aware** that he was ill. cf) unaware: 알지 못하는
14	found	(동) 설립하다 (-founded) He used the money to **found** an internet business. cf) found: find의 과거 I **found** that I could easily swim a mile.
15	afford affordable	(동) (~을 할 경제적, 시간적) 여유가 있다, ~을 할 수 있다 (sth or to do) I can **afford** a new car. I can **afford** to buy a new car. (형) (가격이) 알맞은 (=reasonable) There are few affordable houses in big cities.
16	purchase	① (동) 구매하다 Tickets must be **purchase**d two weeks in advance. ② (명) 구매 How do you wish to pay for your **purchase**s?
17	available	(명) 구할 수 있는, 사용할 수 있는 Is this dress **available** in a larger size?

18	prospective	(형) pro+spect (앞을+보다) → 장래의, 유망한
		DUC Corp. is a **prospective** enterprise.
		cf) '- spect'는 '보다'라는 의미를 갖고 있는 말로 접두사를 무엇을 붙이는 가에 따라 의미가 다른 어휘를 만들 수 있다.
		e.g. re+spect: 다시 보다 → 존경하다
		    in+spect: 안을 보다 → 조사하다
		    retro+spect: 뒤를 보다 → 회고하다
		    pro+spect: 앞을 보다 → 전망, 예상

19	perspective	① (명) 관점, 시각 Try to see the issue from a different **perspective**. ② (명) 원근법 I learnt how to draw a picture in **perspective**. The mountain in the picture is out of **perspective**.
20	establish	(동) 설립하다, 확립하다 The brewery was **establish**ed in 1882.

손님여러분, 저희 비행기는 잠시 후에 _____ 공항에 도착하겠습니다.
저희 승무원들의 착륙준비를 위해 협조해주시기 바라겠습니다.
감사합니다.

Ladies and gentlemen,

we are approaching _____ airport. We will be preparing for the landing. Your cooperation will be appreciated. Thank you.

손님여러분, 우리 비행기는 약 _____ 분 후에 _____ 공항에 도착하겠습니다. 꺼내놓은 짐들은 앞좌석 밑이나 선반 속에 보관해주시기 바라며, 기내 영상물과 음악프로그램을 중단해주시기 바랍니다. 감사합니다.

Ladies and gentlemen,

we are approaching _____ airport. We will arrive _____ airport in _____ minutes. Please store you carry-on items in the overhead beans or under the seat in front of you. Also please end the entertainment program for landing. Thank you for your cooperation.

CHAPTER
11

동명사

동명사란?

나는 노래 **부르는 것**을 좋아한다.
　　　　명사역할

동사 '노래 부르다'가 '노래 부르기', '노래 부르는 것'으로 바뀌어 문장에서 명사 역할을 하는 것을 동명사라고 한다. 동사 뒤에 ing를 붙인 형태!

Tip 명사와 동명사는 무엇이 다른가?

동명사는 목적어를 가질 수 있지만 명사는 목적어를 가질 수 없고, 동명사 앞에는 관사가 올 수 없다.

	동명사	명사
목적어	O	X
관사	X	O
수식	부사 수식을 받음	형용사 수식을 받음

1 동명사의 위치

명사 역할을 하기 때문에 ~하기, ~하는 것으로 해석되며 문장에서 주어, 목적어, 보어 자리와 전치사 바로 뒤에 온다.

ex. **Playing a piano** is one of my hobbies. (주어 자리)

ex. I dislike **getting up early in the morning**. (목적어 자리)

ex. My main interest is **baking the bread**. (보어 자리)

ex. Den left without **saying a word**. (전치사 뒤)

2 동명사 자리에 올 수 없는 것

- 동명사가 와야 하는 주어, 목적어, 보어 자리에 동사나 명사는 올 수 없다.
- 동명사가 와야 하는 전치사 바로 뒷자리에 동사나 to 부정사는 올 수 없다.

✅ Check Up Test

아래 문장에서 문법적 오류를 올바르게 고치시오.

1. <u>Demand</u> a raise in salary is not acceptable.

(→   )

2. The team manager cared about to <u>improve</u> the evaluation form.

(→   )

---

3 동사 + 동명사 ; 동명사만을 목적어로 취하는 동사!

ex. Teenagers **enjoy listening** to music online.

> avoid, admit, consider delay, deny, enjoy, finish, give up, postpone, recommend, suggest, include, reject, quit, discontinue, mind, keep, permit

4 동사 + 동명사 / to 부정사 ; 동명사와 to 부정사를 모두 목적어로 취하는 동사!

ex. They **continued** <u>producing</u> textiles. = They **continued** <u>to produce</u> textiles.

attempt, begin, continue, hate, intend, like, love, prefer, start

Tip "remember, forget, stop"

to 부정사 / 동명사 둘 다 목적어로 취하지만 의미가 달라지는 동사들!

ex. I **remember to meet** him at the bus stop. (미래의 일)

　I **remember meeting** him at the bus stop. (과거의 일)

☞ 해석상 미래의 일을 나타내면 부정사를, 과거의 일을 나타내면 동명사를 선택하라!

forget –ing: 했던 것을 잊다
forget to 부정사: 앞으로 할 일을 잊다

stop –ing: 지금까지 하던 것을 멈추다
stop to 부정사: 무엇을 하기 위해 멈추다

remember –ing: 했던 일을 기억하다
remember to 부정사: 앞으로 할 일을 기억하다

regret –ing: 했던 일을 후회하다
regret to 부정사: ~하게 되어 유감이다

try –ing: 시험 삼아 해보다
try to 부정사: 애써 ~하다

5 동명사의 관용적 표현

be used to ~ing	~에 익숙해지다	= be accustomed to ~ing	~에 익숙해지다
go ~ing	~하러 가다	be busy ~ing	~하는데 바쁘다
be worth ~ing	~할 가치가 있다	be subject to ~ing	~할 가능성이 있다
be opposed to ~ing	~에 반대하다	object to ~ing	~하는 것을 반대하다
be committed to ~ing	~하는 데 전념하다	be devoted to ~ing	~에 몰두하다, 헌신하다
contribute to ~ing	~에 공헌하다, 기여하다	cannot help ~ing	~하지 않을 수 없다
feel like ~ing	~하고 싶다	look forward to ~ing	~을 학수고대하다
spend time(money) ~ ing	~하는 데 시간(돈)을 쓰다	have difficulty (trouble) ~ing	~하는데 어려움을 겪다
insist on ~ing	~할 것을 주장하다	It is no use(good) ~ing	~해도 소용없다
be capable of ~ing	~할 능력이 있다	end up ~ing	결국 ~하다
on ~ing	~하자마자	come close(near) to ~ing	거의 ~할 뻔하다
be aware of ~ing	~을 알고 있다	be skilled at ~ing	~하는 데 능숙하다

(여기서 to는 부정사의 to가 아니다!)

ex. We **look forward to hearing** from you soon.
우리는 당신으로부터 연락받기를 기대합니다.

ex. We **are** fully **committed to preventing** this sort of problem.
다시는 이런 문제가 재발하지 않도록 최선을 다하겠습니다.

01 Ms. Lee is looking forward to _____ Zimmerman, one of the most famous pianists, perform on the stage in Seoul.

(A) see

(B) seeing

(C) be seen

(D) seen

02 Thanks to the intensive training sessions, staff members have no difficulty _____ to the new system.

(A) adopting

(B) adaption

(C) to adapt

(D) adapting

03 In addition to _____ domestic clients, the Majesty Hotel will provide overseas clients with perfect services.

(A) accommodate

(B) accommodation

(C) accommodating

(D) accommodated

04 Please note that all outdoor games are subject to _____ without prior notice.

(A) cancellation

(B) canceling

(C) canceled

(D) cancel

05 _____ usable parts from outdated equipment makes it possible to reduce costs considerably.

(A) Recycled

(B) Recycle

(C) Recycling

(D) Recycles

06 In Monday's regular meeting, Robert Graham, the vice-president, requested that the new project plan be further investigated before _____.

(A) being approved

(B) approving

(C) approve

(D) being approving

07 It is important for businesses to find effective ways of _____ new customers.

(A) attracts

(B) attracting

(C) attraction

(D) attractive

08 The new method of _____ core material from various wild plants for the new medicine is still being tested in the laboratory.

(A) extract

(B) extracting

(C) extracted

(D) being extracted

09 _____ of surveys is not an easy task and requires the help of a computer.

(A) Analyzing

(B) Analyze

(C) Analysis

(D) Analyzed

10 The award-winning movie released yesterday was so moving that all the audience at the movie theater ended up _____ after the movie.

(A) crying

(B) cry

(C) cried

(D) to cry

01 Ms. Lucy has a good chance of _____ a new chief financial officer at DUC Inc.

(A) become　　　　　　　　　　(B) becoming

(C) becomes　　　　　　　　　　(D) will become

02 The management of DUC Inc. is on the process of _____ new guidelines for customer service.

(A) establishing　　　　　　　　(B) establish

(C) to establish　　　　　　　　(D) established

03 Mr. Blaney will be responsible for _____ the firm externally and ensuring that the company has a clear strategic direction in its work.

(A) representing　　　　　　　　(B) representation

(C) represent　　　　　　　　　(D) being represented

04 The planning department is committed to _____ the next week's committee meeting.

(A) arrange　　　　　　　　　　(B) arrange

(C) arrangement　　　　　　　　(D) arranging

05 _____ use the shuttle bus freely, you are advised to sign up in advance and get a transportation card.

(A) Instead of　　　　　　　　　(B) Regard

(C) In order to　　　　　　　　　(D) While

06 Ms. Surrendon is appointed as a chief editor because she has been said to be eligible _____ the editorial department.

(A) leading

(B) leader

(C) to lead

(D) to leading

07 Most of the participants in the seminar spent a lot of time _____ videos, resulting in tremendous complaints.

(A) watching

(B) watched

(C) to watch

(D) watch

08 The Korean public has been _____ to get involved in a Middle Eastern war, just as the Japanese public was.

(A) accustomed

(B) reluctant

(C) opposed

(D) dedicated

09 Suddenly, the team manager told Brian to stop _____ because his words were not appropriate for the presentation

(A) talking

(B) talk

(C) to talk

(D) talked

10 In court, the accountant admitted _____ almost $10 million as consulting fees from the company.

(A) receive

(B) receiving

(C) to receive

(D) receives

손님 여러분, 우리 비행기는 곧 착륙하겠습니다.

좌석 등받이와 발 받침대. 테이블을 제자리로 해주시고, 좌석벨트를 매 주십시오. 창문덮개는 열어 두시기 바라며 비행기가 완전히 멈춘 후 좌석벨트 표시등이 꺼질 때까지 전자기기의 전원을 꺼 주시기 바랍니다.

감사합니다.

Ladies and gentlemen,

We will be landing shortly.

please fasten your seatbelt, return your seat and tray table to the upright position and open your window shades.

Also please discontinue the use of electronic devices until the captain has turned off the seat belt sign.

Thank you.

손님 여러분, 잠시 후 _____ 공항에 도착하겠습니다.

좌석벨트를 매주시고, 좌석 등받이와 테이블, 발받침은 제자리로 해주십시오.

또한 창문 커튼은 열어주십시오. 꺼내놓은 모든 짐은 좌석 아래 혹은 선반 속에 넣어주십시오.

그리고 사용하던 모든 전자제품의 전원을 꺼주시기 바랍니다.

감사합니다.

Ladies and gentlemen,

We will soon land at _____ airport.

Please fasten your seatbelt, and return your seat and tray table to the upright position and open your window shades.

Also put all your belongings in the overhead bins or under the seat and turn off the electronic devices.

Thank you.

CHAPTER
12

분사

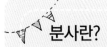

분사란?

잠자는 호랑이
형용사역할

☞ '잠자는'은 호랑이가 잠자고 있는 동작의 의미를 담고 있다. 이처럼 동사의 성질을 갖고 있지만 뒤의 명사를 수식하는 형용사 역할을 하는 것을 분사라고 한다.

1 분사의 형태

현재분사	동사원형 +ing	~한 (능동/진행)
과거분사	동사원형 +ed	~된 (수동/완료)

ex. The boy **playing** basketball is my son.

ex. Those **colored** boxes are mine.

Tip

현재분사 뒤에는 목적어가 올 수 있지만, 과거분사 뒤에는 목적어가 올 수 없다. → 뒤에 목적어가 나온 경우에는 무조건 현재분사가 와야 한다.

ex. The staff **attending the conference** seemed bored.
　　　　　현재분사　　　　　목적어

2 분사는 동사의 성질을 가지고 있다!

분사는 문장에서 동사의 기능을 하지는 않지만 to부정사나 동명사처럼 동사의 성질을 가지고 있다. 따라서 taking pictures처럼 바로 뒤에 목적어나 보어가 올 수 있고, announced yesterday 처럼 부사의 꾸밈을 받기도 한다.

> ex. I know the girl **taking** pictures.
>> 나는 사진 찍고 있는 그 소녀를 안다.

> ex. The news **announced yesterday** surprised us.
>> 어제 발표된 뉴스는 우리를 놀라게 했다.

3 분사자리

형용사 역할을 하므로 형용사처럼!

(1) 명사 앞

뒤 명사와의 관계가 중요하다. 주로 사람 명사 앞은 현재분사, 사물 앞은 과거분사가 오지만 항상 그런 것은 아니다! 반드시 뒤의 명사와의 관계를 생각해보고 해석상 적절한 것을 골라야 한다!

> ex. Ms. Andrea classified the **collected data**.

> ex.

remaining staff	fallen leaves
written contract	broken mirror
revised procedure	limited capacity
attached document	lasting impression

(2) 명사 뒤

- 명사와 분사 사이에 주격 관계대명사 + be동사가 생략된 형태
- 타동사 뒤의 목적어 유무로, 즉 목적어가 있으면 현재분사, 없으면 과거분사

> ex. All students **attending the class** tomorrow should show up for the seminar.

> ex. The building **located** by the bookstore is mine.

(3) 보어 자리

> ex. The export records of last year were **satisfying**.

4 감정표현 동사의 분사형태

disappointing disappointed	interesting interested	surprising surprised
exciting excited	embarrassing embarrassed	confusing confused
satisfied satisfying	boring bored	impressing impressed

5 분사구문이란?

분사를 이용해서 부사절을 간단한 구로 만든 것을 분사구문이라고 한다. '부사구'의 역할을 하며 문장의 앞이나 뒤에 온다.

6 분사구문의 형태

분사구문은 접속사+분사의 형태이다. 부사절 접속사+주어+동사~ 로 되어 있는 부사절을 축약하여 바꾼 것!

　　ex. Because I was tired, I went home early.

　　→ (Being) Tired, I went home early.

　　Tip 분사구문 만드는 방법

　　　　① 부사절 접속사를 생략한다.

　　　　② 부사절의 주어가 주절의 주어와 같은 경우 생략한다.

　　　　③ 부사절의 동사를 현재분사나 과거분사로 바꾼다.

　　　　ex. After she watched a sad movie, she cried.

　　　　→ Watching a sad movie, she cried.

7 분사구문의 주의할 점

(1) 분사구문 앞에 접속사를 남겨놓는 경우도 있다!

– 접속사 생략했을 때 의미가 모호해질 경우

ex. **When** attending the meeting, you have to bring your annual report.

(2) 분사구문의 분사가 와야 하는 자리에 동사나 명사는 올 수 없다!

ex. **Disappointed** at the merger, Mr. Kane quit. (~~Disappointment~~)

→ Because Mr. Kane was disappointed at the merger가 분사구문 Disappointed at the merger 로 바뀜

남자친구가 나를 기다리는 동안에, 그는 음악을 들었다. = 나를 기다리면서, 남자친구는 음악을 들었다.

☞ 두 문장에서 중복되는 부분을 없애고 간단히 표현한 것이다. 영어에서는 중복되는 부분을 없애고 간단히 표현할 때 분사구문을 쓴다.

✅ Check Up Test

1. After _____ encouraged to submit a proposal, Tom decided to conduct a basic study.

   (A) been   (B) being   (C) were   (D) was

2. The school is considering _____ a strict policy regarding student absences.

   (A) to introduce   (B) introduce   (C) introducing   (D) introduced

3. The _____ attractions of the city continue to delight many foreign visitors.

   (A) fascinated   (B) fascinates   (C) fascination   (D) fascinating

---

Tip 분사구문의 부정! 분사구문의 부정은 분사 앞에 not이나 never를 붙인다.

ex. Having money, I can buy the car. → Not having money, I can't buy the car.

8 분사의 관용적인 표현들

① **talking of** / ~에 대해 이야기 하자면

Talking of bears, here is a story for you.

곰에 대해 이야기 하자면 당신에게 해 줄 이야기가 있다.

② **seeing that** / ~을 보면, ~이므로

His English is not bad, seeing that he has learned it for six months.

영어를 배운지 겨우 6개월이라는 것을 감안하면, 그의 영어실력은 나쁘지 않다.

③ **considering** / ~을 고려하면

Considering his age, he sees and hears very well.

나이를 고려하면 그는 잘 보고 잘 듣는다.

④ **compared with** / ~과 비교하면

Compared with last year, prices have risen by 20 percent.

작년과 비교해 물가는 20%가 상승했다.

⑤ **provided(that), providing(that)** / ~라면

Provided (that) all your work is done, you may go home.

Providing (that) all your work is done, you may go home.

일이 다 끝나면 당신은 집에 가도 좋다.

⑥ **generally speaking** / 일반적으로 말해서

Generally speaking, English is not easy to speak.

일반적으로 말해서, 영어는 말하기 쉽지 않다.

① **분사형 전치사 / 접속사**
- regarding, concerning, considering, following, including, excluding, barring, compared with(to), judging from
- provided (that), providing (that), generally (frankly) speaking

② **분사출신의 형용사**
- demanding, existing, challenging, leading, promising, remaining, rewarding
- attached, complicated, designated, detailed, distinguished, experienced, limited, preferred, qualified

01 The new program _____ to start broadcasting in November was abruptly canceled yesterday.

(A) schedule

(B) scheduled

(C) scheduling

(D) to schedule

02 Thanks to Mr. Brown's backup of the computer files, the data in the computer was _____ successfully after the power failure.

(A) recover

(B) recovering

(C) recovered

(D) to recover

03 This year's sales figures were very _____ so the management decided to expand its market overseas.

(A) disappointed

(B) disappoint

(C) disappointing

(D) to disappoint

04 _____ a famous photographer, the magazine will become more popular and make more profits.

(A) Hired

(B) Hire

(C) To hire

(D) Hiring

05 As _____ before, increased prices will be applied to all the products DUC bakery produces.

(A) mention

(B) mentioned

(C) mentioning

(D) mentions

06 DUC Airlines announced that it will offer all employees _____ vacations, a 5% pay rise, professional development courses, and much more.

(A) paying

(B) pay

(C) to pay

(D) paid

07 The fully _____ apartment is conveniently located 5 minutes outside of the subway station and shopping malls.

(A) furnished

(B) furnishing

(C) furniture

(D) furnish

08 Within 2 days, invitations will be e-mailed for a banquet _____ the company's 10th anniversary and welcoming the new CEO.

(A) celebration

(B) celebrating

(C) celebrity

(D) celebrated

09 It is becoming much harder for Pacific Apparel to meet the _____ demand, resulting in hiring more employees.

(A) increase

(B) increased

(C) increases

(D) increasing

10 After _____ to the audience by the CEO, Mr. Lugansky spoke about several financial issues DUC Airline is currently facing and suggested some solutions.

(A) introduced

(B) introducing

(C) introduce

(D) introduction

Grammar Review TEST

01 A recent survey says that more consumers think our product manuals are excessively
_____ .

(A) complicate
(B) complicated
(C) to complicate
(D) complicating

02 As _____ in the rental agreement, the monthly rent of the office should be
transferred to the lessor's account on the last day of each month.

(A) noting
(B) note
(C) notes
(D) noted

03 Since the management of DUC Global Inc. was restructured, the quality of the products
has been much _____ .

(A) improve
(B) to improve
(C) improved
(D) improving

04 _____ a survey conducted by MacMillan Poll, The True Voice reported that around
60% of residents were in favor of renovating the ball park.

(A) To cite
(B) Citation of
(C) Citing
(D) Cited

05 Online orders will be _____ to your address within approximately 2 days of your order.

(A) accustomed
(B) delivered
(C) excited
(D) received

06 It is much too _____ for them to meet the deadline of 2022 project.

(A) uneasy

(B) contentious

(C) demanding

(D) tangled

07 The new CEO will be _____ a speech at the New Year's party on January 1st.

(A) deliver

(B) delivering

(C) delivered

(D) delivery

08 The Blue Book _____ a number of high-quality used cars from compact cars to buses or trucks including motorbikes.

(A) containing

(B) contained

(C) to contain

(D) contains

09 In about 2 months, you may be _____ to participate in another e-mail comsumer survey for Tasty Bakery.

(A) accustomed

(B) committed

(C) asked

(D) interested

10 _____ all around the world, Mr. Godowsky published his new book named Walking into the World, which is nominated for the Book of the Year.

(A) Traveling

(B) Traveled

(C) Having traveled

(D) To have traveled

🎙 기내방송 FAREWELL: GENERAL 1

손님 여러분,

우리 비행기는 인천국제공항에 도착했습니다.

도시명에 오신 것을 환영합니다.

지금 이곳은 12월 1일 월요일 오전오후 9시 20분입니다.

여러분의 안전을 위해 비행기가 완전히 멈춘 후 좌석벨트 표시등이 꺼질 때까지 자리에서 기다려 주십시오. 선반을 여실 때는 안에 있는 물건이 떨어질 수 있으니 조심해 주시고 내리실 때는 잊으신 물건이 없는지 다시 한 번 확인해 주시기 바랍니다. 오늘도 대한항공을 이용해 주셔서 대단히 감사합니다. 저희 승무원들은, 앞으로도 손님 여러분께서 안전하고 편안하게 여행하실 수 있도록 최선을 다하겠습니다. 감사합니다. 안녕히 가십시오.

Ladies and gentlemen,

We have landed at Incheon International Airport.

The local time is now 9:20 a.m/p.m. month / date.

For your safety, please remain seated until the captain has returned off the seat belt sign. Also, please be careful when opening the overhead bins as the contents may fall out. Please remember to take all of your belongings with you when you leave the airplane. Thank you for choosing Korean Air, a member of the SkyTeam alliance and we hope to see you again soon on your next flight.

Airline TOEIC Intro
Essential TOEIC &
Cabin Crew English

접속사와 전치사

접속사란?

이 딸기는 달다. **그리고** 상큼하다.

☞ 두 문장이 '그리고'로 연결되는 것과 같이 단어와 단어, 구와 구 또는 절과 절을 연결하는 것을 접속사라고 한다.

1 접속사의 종류

접속사	**등위접속사**	and	그리고
		but	그러나
		or	또는
		so	그래서
		yet	그러나
	상관접속사	both A and B	A와 B 둘 다
		either A or B	A 또는 B
		neither A nor B	A도 B도 아닌
		not only A but also B	A뿐만 아니라 B도
	종속접속사	명사절 접속사	that(~라는 것), if/whether(~인지) 등
		부사절 접속사	because(~이기 때문에), although(비록~이지만), when, after 등
		형용사절 접속사(=관계대명사)	who(~하는 사람), which(~하는 것) 등

2 등위접속사

단어나 구, 절을 대등하게 이어주는 접속사! 이 중에 서로 짝을 이루어 써야 하는 접속사를 상관접속사라고 부른다.

ex. I opposed her view **but** accepted it.

ex. We will watch **either** a play **or** a movie.

3 종속접속사

주절과 종속절로 이루어진 문장에서 종속절을 이끄는 접속사!

    ex. Ann was late for the interview **because** there was a traffic jam. (부사절접속사)

∗ 명사절 접속사: '절'이 명사 역할을 하여 문장에서 주어, 목적어, 보어 자리에 오도록 이끄는 것

    ex. Mr. Lee has not decided **whether he will be transferred.**

∗ 부사절 접속사: '절'이 부사 역할을 하여 주절을 수식하도록 이끄는 것

    ex. **Although Tom is inexperienced**, he did his best.

시간부사절	after(~후에), before(~전에), when/as(~할 때), as soon as(~하자마자), since(~한 이래로), until(~까지), once(일단 ~하면), by the time(that)(~할 때 즈음), while(~하는 동안에)
목적부사절	so that(~할 수 있도록), in order that(~할 수 있도록)
양보부사절	though/although(~이기는 하지만), even if/even though(비록~일지라도)
조건부사절	unless(만약~하지 않으면), if(만약~한다면), provided/providing(that)(만약~한다면), suppose/supposing(that)(만약~한다면), as(so) long as(~하는 한), in case(that)(~하는 경우에)
원인부사절	because(~ 때문에), since(~ 때문에), as(~ 때문에), now that(~ 때문에)

∗ 형용사절 접속사: '절'이 명사를 수식하는 형용사 역할을 하도록 이끄는 것

    ex. We released a new book **which is about airline service.**

Tip 접속사 that과 관계대명사 what의 구분문제 자주 출제!

ex. I argue that he is one of the criminals. [that뒤에는 완벽한 절]

ex. What I need is money. [what 뒤에는 need의 목적어가 없는 불완전한 절]

단! that이 관계대명사일 때는 뒤에 불완전한 구조가 온다!

ex. Field hockey is a team sport that is played throughout the world. [that이하 절은 주어가 생략된 형태]

Check Up Test

1. _____ annual health check-ups are helpful, it is not a requirement.

   (A) And   (B) Who

   (C) Which   (D) Although

2. Profits rose not _____ because of an increase in sales, but also a reduction in expenses.

   (A) alone   (B) only

   (C) over   (D) less

전치사란?

명사나 대명사 앞에서 시간, 장소, 방향 등을 나타내는 것

   # 전치사 뒤에 형용사나 동사는 올 수 없다!

   ex. The city hall is **under** <u>construction</u>. [~~constructive~~]

전치사의 종류

의미	시간 전치사	at, for
	장소 전치사	in, between
	방향 전치사	to, across
	기타 전치사	목적/수단/이유 전치사

| 형태 | 한 단어 전치사 | on, under, for, since |
| | 두 단어 이상인 전치사 | due to, instead of, in front of, in addition to |

✔ Check Up Test

1. The employees who recently joined the cs team were referred to you for _____ .

   (A) guide　　　　(B) guided　　　　(C) guidance　　　　(D) guidable

2. You had better present you ideas _____ your supervisor.

   (A) for　　　　(B) at　　　　(C) to　　　　(D) of

1 시간 전치사

	at	시각·시점 앞	at 9 o'clock, at noon/night/midnight
~(때)에	on	날짜·요일·특정한 날 앞	on March 2, on New Year's Day
	in	연도·월·계절·오전/오후/저녁 앞	in 2013, in March, in the morning
~동안에	for	for+기간(숫자) ; 며칠/몇 년 등	I worked in marketing for two years.
	during	during+특정기간 ; 휴가/방학 등	I traveled abroad during my vacation.
~까지	until	상황이 계속되다가 그 시점에 종료	The bank is open until 4 pm.
	by	마감이나 기한 표현	You have to come back by 11pm.

Tip 부사어는 시간전치사와 함께 쓸 수 없다!

this, next, last, tomorrow, yesterday, every, that way를 전치사 in, on, at과 같이 쓰면 중복 오류

ex. She visited the international office ~~in every day~~. → every day.

ex. We have been really busy ~~in this week~~. → this week.

2 장소 전치사

above	~보다 위에
below	~보다 아래에
in front of	~앞에
behind	~뒤에
round	~을 돌아서
around	~주위에, ~둘레에
beside/next to/by	~옆에
beneath	표면~밑에
over	~바로 위에
under	~바로 아래에

3 방향 전치사

to	~에게, ~로
toward	~쪽으로, ~을 향하여
across	~을 가로질러
through	~을 통과하여
along	~을 따라
into	~안으로
out of	~밖으로

✅ **Check Up Test**

1. The shopping mall will be relocated _____ the main city hall next year.

  (A) near   (B) of   (C) after   (D) side

2. He attended a really interesting conference _____ weekend on how to expand the domestic market.

  (A) last   (B) at last   (C) in last   (D) on last

Tip 접속사와 전치사는 뭐가 다른가?

접속사는 절(문장)을 이끌고, 전치사는 구나 단어를 이끈다!

ex. We have helped over 50 or phanages <u>since 10 years ago</u>. (전치사)

ex. We have helped over 50 or phanages <u>since we had established our company in 10 years ago</u>. (접속사)

접속사	전치사
although, (even) though	in spite of, despite
because, since, as	because of, due to, owing to
unless	without, except
while	during
if, in case (that)	in case of

01 _____ the new computer was not working well, it was shipped back to the seller right away.

(A) For

(B) In spite of

(C) Because

(D) Until

02 _____ a number of inquiries from the reporters, Steve Kim announced STK Inc. will invest more in research and development in the coming year.   .

(A) Following

(B) While

(C) Against

(D) Though

03 You will probably receive the official invitation with more details _____ the end of the week.

(A) to

(B) by

(C) in

(D) on

04 Close interactions with financial experts inside and outside of the company are necessary to deal with this situation.

(A) only

(B) both

(C) nor

(D) any

05 _____ impressed the audience most was the comfort of the seating at the DUC movie theater.

(A) Those

(B) That

(C) When

(D) What

06 No one is allowed to enter the hall _____ the concert.

(A) while   (B) when

(C) during   (D) for

07 One recent survey says _____ around 60% of young people spend more than 3 hours visiting other SNSs or updating their ones.

(A) for   (B) what

(C) whether   (D) that

08 There is some doubt as to _____ the virus is dangerous and deadly.

(A) that   (B) what

(C) how   (D) whether

09 Club members are allowed to attend all the events held by DUC Club _____ no cost.

(A) by   (B) until

(C) at   (D) from

10 Moving costs are much higher during the summer months _____ the volume of shipment handled by your moving company tends to increase.

(A) for   (B) where

(C) if   (D) when

01 It is our policy that the customer service representatives at DUC Systems return customer calls _____ an hour.

(A) but

(B) within

(C) for

(D) or

02 Mr. Cheng is considering _____ to participate in the Beijing World Robot Competition as his robot has not been completed yet.

(A) whether

(B) about

(C) that

(D) after

03 The person _____ job is to design or build things such as roads, railways, bridges, or machines is an engineer.

(A) what

(B) her

(C) whose

(D) this

04 All construction work must be carried out _____ with strict safety regulations.

(A) in compliance

(B) complied

(C) comply

(D) compliant

05 _____ the last decade, Luen Community Center has been recognized as the most reliable re-education facility in the area.

(A) Throughout

(B) At

(C) While

(D) Beside

06 Part-time workers at LeBlack restaurant are overworked _____ underpaid.

(A) however

(B) who

(C) but

(D) and

07 No matter _____ attractive, any proposal will not be accepted without permission by Chunk Taylor, the new CFO.

(A) how

(B) what

(C) that

(D) whose

08 _____ having experienced declines in revenue during the last quarter, DUC Engineering Inc. is trying to hire 2 more financial experts next quarter.

(A) If

(B) Despite

(C) What

(D) For

09 DUC Motors _____ labor union has voted on a strike for a pay raise is making every effort to mediate a settlement.

(A) whatever

(B) whose

(C) who

(D) which

10 _____ the real estate market and the banking industry saw a sharp decrease in profits over the past 3 years.

(A) All

(B) None

(C) Both

(D) Either

	필수어휘	의미 및 예문
1	deadline	(명) 마감시간, 마감일 It will be difficult to meet the **deadline**.
2	retire	(동) (정년이 되어) 은퇴하다 He is due to **retire** as chief executive next year.

3	resign	(동) 사임하다 (=quit)
		He **resigned** from the company in order to take a more challenging job.
		cf) "해고하다"
		① 잘못으로 인한 해고
		    A dismiss B → B is/get dismissed
		    A fire B B is/get fired
		    A sack B B is/get sacked
		② 어쩔 수 없이 당하는 해고
		    A restructure B → B is/get restructured
		    A lay off B B is/get laid off
		    A make B redundant (잉여적인)
		        → B is/get made redundant

4	questionnaire	(명) 설문지 Please fill in the **questionnaire**. cf) survey: (설문) 조사 A recent **survey** shows unemployment rate has dropped dramatically.
5	constraint	(명) 제약 Financial **constraint**s on the company are preventing them from employing new staff.
6	carrier	(명) 항공사, 운송회사, 배달원 He got a job as a mail **carrier**.
7	career	(명) 직업, 경력 She started her **career** as a pilot.
8	courier	(명) 택배사, 배달원 We can send the document by **courier**.
9	profit	(명) 수익 She makes a big **profit** from selling waste material to textile companies.
10	position	(명) 위치, 직위, 일자리 My financial **position** is somewhat precarious at the moment. [precarious: 불안정한, 위태위태한]

필수어휘	의미 및 예문
11 issue	(명) 문젯거리, 주제, (잡지 등) 호 Money is not a big **issue**. There's an article on motorbikes in the next **issue**. (동) 발표하다, 발행하다 The office will be **issu**ing permits on Tuesday mornings.
12 fare	(명) (교통) 요금 Train **fare**s are going up again.
13 promote	(동) pro+mote (앞으로+움직이다) → 승진시키다, 홍보하다 She's jest been **promote**d to senior sales rep. [rep.: representative (직원)] Advertising companies are always having to think up new ways to **promote** products.
14 additional	(형) 추가적인, 부가적인 There will be an extra charge for any **additional** passengers.
15 relevant related	(형) 관련 있는 (to) Education should be **relevant** to the child's needs. (형) (어떤 식으로든) 연관된 We discussed unemployment and **related** issues.
16 adequate	(형) 충분한, 적절한 Have we got **adequate** food for 20 guests? cf) inadequate: 충분하지 않은, 부적절한
17 worth	(형) ~의 가치가 있는 This car is **worth** about $5,000. This museum is certainly **worth** a visit.
18 due	① (형) ~때문에, ~로 인해 (to) A lot of her unhappiness is **due** to boredom. cf) 원래 due라는 형용사는 'resulting (~로 결론 나는)" 이라는 의미를 가지고 　　있어서 전치사 'to'와 의미적으로 잘 어울려 결국 'due to'가 하나의 　　전치사처럼 '~로 인해, ~덕분에'라는 뜻을 가지게 되었다. ② (형) (~하기로) 예정된 The next meeting is **due** to be held in three months' time.
19 competent	(명) 능숙한, 능력 있는 (=skilled) I wouldn't say he was brilliant but he is **competent** at his job. cf) incompetent: 능숙하지 않은
20 competitive	(형) 경쟁적인 You're very **competitive** – it's meant to be a friendly match! cf) competitive prices/services

손님 여러분,

우리 비행기는 (　　) 공항에 도착했습니다.

지금 이곳은 (　　) 월 (　　) 일 오전_{오후} ____시 ____분입니다.

비행기가 완전히 멈춘 후, 좌석벨트 표시등이 꺼질 때까지 잠시만 자리에서 기다려 주십시오.

선반을 여실 때는 안에 있는 물건이 떨어질 수 있으니 조심해 주시고 내리실 때는 잊으신 물건이 없는지 다시 한 번 살펴주십시오. 오늘도 (　　) 항공을 이용해 주셔서 대단히 감사합니다. 저희 승무원들은, 앞으로도 손님 여러분께서 안전하고 편안하게 여행하실 수 있도록 최선을 다하겠습니다. 즐거운 여행이 되시기 바랍니다. 감사합니다. 안녕히 가십시오.

Ladies and gentlemen,

We have landed at 공항명 International Airport.

The local time is now (___:___) a.m/p.m. month / date.

For your safety, please remain seated until the captain has returned off the seat belt sign. When you open the overhead bins, be careful as the contents may fall out. And also please have all you belongings with you when you deplane. Thank you for choosing (   ) Airline, and we hope to see you again soon on your next flight. We wish you a pleasant stay hear in 도시명. Thank you.

CHAPTER
14

관계대명사와
관계부사

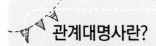

관계대명사란?

관계대명사에는 who, which, that 등이 있다. 앞에 나온 명사가 사람, 사물인지, 문장 내에서 주격, 목적격, 소유격으로 쓰이는지에 따라 각각 다른 관계대명사가 쓰인다.

	주격	목적격	소유격
사람	who	who / whom	whose
사물, 동물	which	which	whose / of which
사람, 사물, 동물	that	that	–

ex. Olivia mentioned a former **colleague who** quit his job last year.
[주격관계대명사]

1 관계대명사 주의사항

→ 목적격 관계대명사는 전치사의 목적어가 될 수 있다. 단 that 앞에는 전치사를 사용할 수 없다.

ex. This is the colleague **with whom** you can discuss your progress.

[전치사가 관계대명사 앞에 위치할 경우에는 who가 아닌 목적격 whom을 써야 한다.]

→ 관계대명사 앞에 오는 전치사는 종속절의 동사 또는 전치사구와 밀접한 관련이 있다. 관용적으로 사용하는 숙어나 전치사구에 주목할 필요가 있다.

ex. Employees should inform their manager when working in an isolated place **with which** they are not familiar.

[be familiar with ~에 낯익다]

관계부사란?

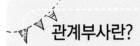

관계부사는 접속사와 부사의 역할을 하며, 형용사절 _{한정사가 있을 경우} 또는 명사절 _{한정사가 없는 경우} 을 이끈다.

> 내가 좋아하는 가수
> ☞ '내가 좋아하는'과 같이 명사를 꾸며주는 절을 형용사절이라고 하고, 형용사절 접속사는 관계대명사라고 부르기도 한다.

2 관계부사의 기능

ex. This is the company, **and there** I worked as a researcher.

→ This is the company **where** I worked as a researcher.

관계부사의 선행사	관계부사	전치사+관계대명사
시간(day, year, time)	when / that	at / in / on which
장소(area, place, building)	where / that	at / in / on which
이유(the reason)	why / that	for which
방법(the way)을 나타내는 어구	how / that	in which

Tip the way 와 how는 같이 쓸 수 없다.

ex. It is my pleasure to explain **how** one of our stores typically functions. [= in which]

ex. Please tell me **the reason why** you applied for this position. [= for which]

01 The movie is based on the novel _____ was written by Neila Graham.

  (A) what   (B) which

  (C) when   (D) who

02 The shopping mall is near the subway station, _____ makes it easy for shoppers to access the mall.

  (A) which   (B) what

  (C) who   (D) whom

03 It is necessary for people _____ work under a lot of pressure to exercise on a regular basis and maintain a well-balanced diet.

  (A) where   (B) whoever

  (C) when   (D) who

04 DUC Mecenat is a non-profit organization _____ mission is to discover and support prominently talented artists around the world.

  (A) whose   (B) what

  (C) that   (D) where

05 Of all the business plans _____ by the sales manager, Ms. Aselin's idea is the most impressive and persuasive.

  (A) reviewed   (B) which reviewed

  (C) reviewing   (D) are reviewed

06 All the residents of this apartment are required to avoid the underground parking lot _____ the floor is being repaved.

(A) how

(B) with which

(C) which

(D) where

07 Mr. Baek is offering a two-hour seminar during _____ he will share some perspectives on efficient personnel management.

(A) that

(B) this

(C) which

(D) what

08 Interstate 78, _____ there was a car accident, was completely closed for many hours.

(A) where

(B) on that

(C) which

(D) for which

09 DUC Design Inc. has 10 web designers, some of _____ are highly skilled designers with at least 10 years of experience.

(A) which

(B) that

(C) them

(D) whom

10 When the foreign vendors visited The Cloud Nine restaurant, _____ were served a special dish with a premium wine.

(A) which

(B) where

(C) they

(D) that

01 Robert called the seller yesterday in order to ask about the invoice number of the TV set _____ was ordered 2 days ago.

(A) whoever (B) that

(C) who (D) of which

02 City Bank customers are requested to update regularly their passwords _____ use for Internet banking.

(A) which (B) they

(C) that (D) who

03 The new call-in TV show, _____ which viewers can freely participate in the program on the phone, will begin airing at 7 p.m. next Monday.

(A) during (B) at

(C) even (D) while

04 The gardening tool set _____ ordered two days ago is currently out of stock.

(A) you (B) which

(C) who (D) it

05 The historical building, _____ roof was recently repainted, is one of the major tourist attractions in this area.

(A) which (B) whose

(C) of which (D) where

06 _____ completes the survey will be offered a 10% discount coupon for any menus La Fleur Restaurant provides .

(A) Whom

(B) What

(C) That

(D) Whoever

07 Be aware that candidates _____ applications are incomplete will not be considered for an interview.

(A) her

(B) whom

(C) whose

(D) that

08 You can order our products either online or in person, _____ is easier and more convenient.

(A) what

(B) it

(C) whoever

(D) whichever

09 Those _____ in this special winter outdoor activity program must visit our homepage and sign up in advance.

(A) who are interested

(B) who interest

(C) interesting

(D) who have interested

10 The senior manager of human resources department interviewed a lot of candidates but none of _____ had acceptable qualifications for the job.

(A) which

(B) them

(C) whom

(D) that

필수어휘	의미 및 예문
1 temporary	(형) 임시의, 일시적인 She has managed to obtain a **temporary** residence permit. cf) permanent: 영구의
2 permanent	(형) 영구의, 영원한 Are you looking for a temporary or a permanent job? cf) perm: permanent wave (파마)
3 construction	(명) con+struct (함께+쌓아올리다) → 건설 (셀 수 없음), 건축물 (셀 수 있음) The tower is a marvelous work of engineering and **construction**. This house is a simple wooden **construction**.
4 revise	(동) re+vise (다시+보다) → 수정하다, 개정하다, 변경하다 His publishers made him **revise** his manuscript three times. [**manuscript**: manu (손) + scribe (쓰다) → 원고]
5 renovation	(명) 수리, 혁신, 리모델링 The museum is closed for **renovation**.
6 succeed	① (동) 성공하다 (in) She's been trying to pass her driving test for six years and she's finally **succeeded**. cf) (형) successive: 연속적인 　　(명) succession: 연속, 연쇄 ② (동) (~의) 뒤를 잇다, 승계하다 He **succeeded** his father as editor of the paper. cf) (형) successful: 성공적인 　　(명) success: 성공
7 brief	(동) (시간) 짧은, (말/글) 간단한 The company issued a **brief** statement about yesterday's accident.
8 replace	(동) re+place (다시+놓다) → 교체하다, 대체하다, 대신하다 The factory **replace**d most of its workers with robots.
9 opportunity	(명) 기회 (=chance) The exhibition is a unique **opportunity** to see her later work. [work: 작품] cf) chance와 opportunity는 거의 비슷하게 사용될 수 있는 표현이다. e.g. I got a chance to do something. 　　 I got an opportunity to do something. 하지만, chance는 불확실하게 '실패에 대한 위험성(risk of failure)'을 내포하고 있다. 반면에 opportunity는 chance보다는 긍정적인 의미로 '목표나 바람이 있어서 그런 와중에 생긴 기회'라는 의미로 '뭔가 이득이 될 만한 기회'를 의미한다. 그래서, taking a chance와 taking an opportunity는 다르다. Taking a chance는 '실패를 염두에 두고 무언가를 한다'는 의미고 taking an opportunity는 '어떻게든 현재 상황에서 나에게 이득이 될 만한 무언가를 한다' 라고 해석할 수 있다.

	필수어휘	의미 및 예문
10	personnel	(명) (조직의) 구성원, 인사과 The new director is likely to make major changes in **personnel**. cf) personal: (형) 개인적인
11	HR (Human Resources)	(명) 인적자원 (=personnel), 인사과 China is rich in **human resources**.
12	line up	(동) 줄을 서다, 한 줄로 정렬하다 Thousands of people **lined up** to buy tickets on opening night. cf) line-up: (특정행사) 참석자들, (사물의) 목록
13	load	(동) 짐을 싣다 How long will it take to **load** this sand onto the lorry? cf) unload: 짐을 내리다 overload: 과적하다
14	approximately	(부) 거의, 대략 The job will take **approximately** three weeks, and cost **approximately** $1,000.
15	in operation	(부) 사용중인, 가동중인 The air-conditioner is now **in operation**.
16	job opening	(명) 구인 There aren't many suitable **job openings** out there for me. cf) '자리가 열려있다'는 뜻에서 사용이 되는 말로 흔히 빈자리를 T.O.라고 많이 하는데 이건 잘못된 표현이고 job opening 혹은 job vacancy라고 한다.
17	video-conference	(명) 화상회의 (동) 화상회의 하다 We will be **videoconferencing** with our clients this morning.
18	consult consultation consultant	(동) (~와) 상담하다 If the symptoms get worse, consult your doctor. [symptom: 증상] (명) 상담, 협의, 진찰 After **consultation** with our accountants, we've decided how to cut costs within the company. (명) 상담사, 자문위원 The former general now serves as a **consultant** to the Pentagon.
19	acclaim	(동) 환호하다, 극찬하다 (=praise) She was publicly **acclaim**ed for her contribution to the discovery.
20	accommodate accommodation accommodations	(동) (지낼) 공간을 제공하다, 수용하다 New students may be **accommodate**d in halls of residence. (명) (살거나, 일하거나, 머물)거처, 공간 (단수) There's a shortage of cheap **accommodation**. (명) 숙소, 숙박시설 (복수) They paid for her flights and hotel **accommodations**.

(   ) 항공에서 손님 여러분께 안내 말씀드리겠습니다. 지금 (   ) 인하여 탑승수속이 지연되고 있습니다. 잠시만 기다려 주시기 바랍니다. 불편을 끼쳐드려 죄송합니다.

May I have you attention, please. The check-in process is temporarily delayed due to (   ). We feel sorry for this inconvenience and we will keep you informed of further notice. We really appreciate your cooperation.

기내방송 출발 지연 안내

(　　) 항공에서 (　　)로 출국하시는 손님 여러분께 안내 말씀드리겠습니다. (　　) 항공
＿＿ 시 ＿＿ 분 편이 (　　)로 인하여 정시보다 (　　) 분이 지연되어 ＿＿ 시 ＿＿ 분에
출발예정입니다. 널리 양해해주시기 바랍니다.

May I have you attention, please. (　　) Airline flight (　　) bound for 도시명 at ＿＿ :
＿＿ will be delayed for (　　) hours and (　　) minutes due to (　　). The new departure
time is ＿＿ : ＿＿ . We are very sorry for this inconvenience and your understanding will
be appreciated.

Appendix

실전 예상문제

101 The tile samples _____ back to the manufacturer when a number of the tiles delivered were defective.

(A) send

(B) sent

(C) being sent

(D) were sent

102 Sales revenue _____ dramatically since the company's new ad was aired on TV.

(A) increase

(B) which increases

(C) has increased

(D) increasing

103 The manager would like to thank the workers for the highest _____ the company has had in the last 10 years.

(A) product

(B) produce

(C) productive

(D) productivity

104 It is very important to clearly state and define the _____ of the project before planning the first stage.

(A) objective

(B) objection

(C) object

(D) objectivity

105 Some employees at Bristol Inc. prefer working in an open-plan office while _____ want to work in a private place.

(A) another

(B) the others

(C) other

(D) one

106 Employers should make it routine _____ the strong points of each employee in order to motivate them.

(A) access

(B) to access

(C) accessing

(D) accessed

107 _____ creating a consensus, the board members asked that the decision be postponed.

(A) Failed

(B) When they fail

(C) Having failed

(D) failing

108 _____ important information for the next conference will be available from our Web site or in person.

(A) Those

(B) Another

(C) Other

(D) Every

109 Applicants for the director position must be _____ to work and live in Tokyo.

(A) prior

(B) applicable

(C) eligible

(D) convenient

110 Mr. Sanchez's skills in _____ computer programming and graphic design make him a competitive candidate.

(A) either

(B) neither

(C) both

(D) most

111 The upcoming seminar will explain _____ small company can create a unique brand image that everybody in the world can know well.

(A) whether

(B) how

(C) what

(D) which

112 The office supplies for the billing department _____ kept in room 121, next to the conference room B.

(A) to be

(B) is

(C) being

(D) are

113 If you _____ to see a complete list of the candidates, please contact Mr. Kim in the personnel department.

(A) wish

(B) will wish

(C) wished

(D) are wished

114 It is possible to complete our marketing research by tomorrow only if we work together _____ .

(A) productive

(B) productivity

(C) productively

(D) productiveness

115 Here at DUC Restaurant, we believe that personal hygiene is _____ important as the food taste.

(A) more

(B) as

(C) similarly

(D) much

116 Visitors to the constructions site should be _____ that they must be equipped with protective gear.

(A) afraid

(B) aware

(C) aligned

(D) awake

117 Adrian Bolsher will discuss the yearly budget with the team members when they _____ formally next week.

(A) will meet

(B) met

(C) have met

(D) meet

118 Speaking _____ behalf of the CEO, Malcolm thanked the employees for their dedicated contribution to the new project.

(A) for

(B) in

(C) as

(D) on

119 In accordance with a report _____ by the National Bureau of Transportation, driving with the headlights on increases safety.

(A) published

(B) publish

(C) publishing

(D) to publish

120 The president of DUC Cosmetics is considering _____ the company headquarter to Busan.

(A) to relocate

(B) has relocated

(C) relocation

(D) relocating

121 In Mr. Kwon's absence, all inquiries _____ the new marketing strategy should be directed to his assistant.

(A) assuming

(B) pertaining

(C) concerning

(D) regardless of

122 DUC Printing's profits have risen _____ since the company introduced a new cutting-edge printing machine.

(A) occasionally

(B) competitively

(C) steadily

(D) nearly

123 The sales figure in this quarter is much higher than _____ in the previous quarter.

(A) this

(B) that

(C) those

(D) it

124 The planning department will decide _____ or not to hire more part-time workers for the pop-up store.

(A) whether

(B) that

(C) if

(D) either

125 Prinston Shipping _____ to take this opportunity to thank you for the work your company has done.

(A) has liked

(B) liked

(C) will like

(D) would like

126 All orders for office supplies must _____ to Mr. Brown by Friday at 5 p.m.

(A) submit

(B) be submitting

(C) be submitted

(D) submitted

127 While the marketing department is temporarily closed, all orders will be _____ by the general affairs department.

(A) expired

(B) replied

(C) handled

(D) attended

128 Neither taking pictures _____ eating or drinking is allowed during the performance in this theater.

(A) and

(B) nor

(C) or

(D) but

129 We are pleased to announce that Alan _____ his new position as web designer and graphic designer on February 1st.

(A) will be starting

(B) has been starting

(C) was started

(D) is being started

130 Matthew Leblanc's achievements in psychology were remarkable, _____ considering that he was only twenty years old at the time.

(A) greatly

(B) unusually

(C) positively

(D) especially

Airline TOEIC Intro
Essential TOEIC &
Cabin Crew English

| 저자 소개 | ✈

강혜순

- 버펄로 뉴욕주립대학교. TESOL 석사
- 고려대학교 일반대학원 영어학 박사
- 세종대학교 일반대학원 관광경영학 박사
- 대림대학교 국제교류원 원장 역임
- 대림대학교 항공호텔관광학부 학부장 역임

Airline TOEIC Intro

초판 1쇄 인쇄	2021년 2월 25일
초판 1쇄 발행	2021년 3월 2일

저　자	강혜순
펴낸이	임순재
펴낸곳	**(주)한올출판사**
등　록	제11-403호
주　소	서울시 마포구 모래내로 83(한올빌딩 3층)
전　화	(02) 376-4298(대표)
팩　스	(02) 302-8073
홈페이지	www.hanol.co.kr
e-메일	hanol@hanol.co.kr
ISBN	979-11-6647-059-2